TOO LATE?

by
John M. Haffert

Published in the USA by QUEEN OF THE WORLD CENTER

National Office	*Eastern Office*	*Publication Office*
PO Box 20870	545 74th Street	PO Box 50
Wichita, KS 67208	Brooklyn, NY 11209	Asbury, NJ 08802

Published in ASIA by   *INTERNATIONAL CENTER*
BAHAY MARIA   SEDES MUNDI REGINAE
95 Ampola Street   Ao Castelo
Bel-Air 3, Makati City   Ourem
Philippines   Portugal

Distributed in the U.S.A. by:
The 101 Foundation, Inc.
P.O. Box 151
Asbury, NJ 08802

Phone: (908) 689-8792
Fax: (908) 689-1957
www.101foundation.com
e-mail: 101@101foundation.com

ISBN: 1-890137-39-1

CONTENTS

APPENDIX

FOREWORD

by Honorable Howard Q. Dee

I n May 1981, while researching the Fatima message, I came
across a commemorative text concerning Fatima which
had just been broadcast over Radio Vatican. In part it said:

*Neither Pope John XXIII nor Pope Paul VI, considered
it advisable to reveal to the world the third part of the secret
of Fatima. However it is certain that the third part of the
Secret is of particular gravity. Have we reached a fullness
of times? Are we living the beginning of the Apocalypse
prophesied by St. John?*

*The time has come when words are not enough anymore.
It is now necessary to act immediately if we wish that
humanity, that each of us, may be able to see, beside the
fire, the light.*

I was stunned. Why was the authoritative and conser-
vative Radio Vatican referring to fire and apocalyptic times?
I sensed the Holy See was issuing a wake-up call.

Mary's Rightful Place

This is what I believe: Mary's rightful place beside Jesus
needs to be established to prepare for the fulfillment of a
promise made by Our Lady at Fatima, which was the
conversion of Russia and a time of world peace. It is the
long awaited Triumph of Her Immaculate Heart promised
at Fatima that will bring peace to all nations. The entire
Catholic world, led by the Holy Father, is anticipating and
yearning for this victory.

Tied together with this victory are three messages of the
twentieth century—Fatima, Amsterdam, and Akita—guiding
the destiny of mankind in the new millennium.

Fatima occurred in 1917. Twenty-eight (28) years after
Fatima, in 1945, Our Lady of All Nations came to Amsterdam.
After another 28 years, She manifested Herself in Akita,
Japan. Another 28 years will bring us to the first year of
the third millennium, 2001.

Bishop John Ito, Ordinary of Akita who approved the
apparitions, wrote to me after he briefed the Holy Father

about the Akita events and presented his pastoral to Cardinal Joseph Ratzinger for approval. Bishop Ito was certain that Akita was an extension of Fatima. And Cardinal Ratzinger personally confirmed to me that these two messages, of Fatima and Akita, are essentially the same.

Necessary to Act Immediately

We must heed the advice of Radio Vatican given in May, 1981 (at the time of the attempted assassination of the Pope): "The time has come when words are not enough anymore. *It is now necessary to act immediately if we wish that humanity, that each of us, may be able to see, besides the fire, the light.*"

Two thousand years ago the Holy Spirit came upon Mary, and when the power of the Most High overshadowed Her, She conceived Jesus, Son of God. Now it is the Mother of all Nations, the Coredemprix, Mediatrix of all Grace and Advocate, who will accompany Her Spouse to descend into our hearts and souls and recreate in each of us—if we give *our* fiat—the likeness of Jesus.

United with the Hearts of Jesus and Mary, in Their passion for the Father's Will, with the fire of the Holy Spirit blazing in us, we can dispel the darkness that shrouds the world and renew the face of the earth.

Ambassador Dee with the Holy Father. For a more comprehensive statement, see the Nov. 1998 edition of *Inside the Vatican.* Authorizing this foreword, his Excellency said: "Let us pray it is not too late."

"Several entire nations will be annihilated... To prevent this... If my requests are heard... My Immaculate Heart will triumph and an era of peace will be granted to mankind..."

– Our Lady of Fatima

"I have today set before you life and prosperity, death and doom... Choose life, then, that you and your descendants may live by loving the Lord your God, heeding His voice..."

– Exhortation of Moses
Deut. 30:15-20

"O how wonderful it will be to hear Our Lady hailed QUEEN OF THE WORLD. It will be a time of peace, joy, and well being, which will last a long time."

– St. Catherine Laboure

"It will be a time of great joy when Mary, as Mistress and Queen of Hearts, is enthroned."

– St. Grignion de Montfort

CHAPTER ONE

TOO LATE FOR RWANDA

The world was shocked to learn that in Rwanda over 500,000 people were brutally killed by their own neighbors.

The world would be far more shocked if it realized that God gave Rwanda a warning. The tragedy could have been prevented. *And something even worse is now predicted for each one of us.*

Most know through press reports about the brutal slaughter in Rwanda. Very few, however, seem aware that ten years before the massacre, the Blessed Virgin appeared to warn them and to give *specific requests to avoid a "river of blood."*

Her requests were not heard. And the warning message She had given came true to the letter: **"A river of blood ...people killing each other...bodies without their heads."**

Many of the half million who died were beheaded.

Equivalent to *25 Million* Killed in U.S.

To understand the magnitude of this, relative to the population of Rwanda, the half million killed there would be equivalent in the United States to the mass slaying of TWENTY FIVE MILLION.

And this horror, which literally staggers the imagination, is not over. It will not be over for years to come.

Many of us entered the third millennium with so much hope. At the same time, the 175,000 arrested for the massacre were crowded in small cells—as many as seventy in an area fifteen feet square—while only four judges were hearing their cases. Most of them would probably die in jail. Counting members of their families (parents, brothers and sisters, children, grandchildren), the extended suffering greatly exceeded the half million who were killed.

Why Didn't the Catholics Listen?

Since many Rwandans are Catholic, why did they ignore the warning given them by the Mother of Heaven?

I was asked in 1982, at the time of the visions in Rwanda, to translate the messages into English. I wrote to the local bishop to know whether the apparitions were credible. *He answered that they were.*

22,000 Rwandans saw the visionaries cry out, as Our Lady described what was going to happen, during apparitions which lasted continuously over a period of many weeks. And then, they had *ten years* to respond.

What must be most chilling for *us* is that Our Lady said in Rwanda *that She came for the entire world.* She said:

"I am concerned not only for Rwanda or for the whole of Africa. I am concerned with, and turning to, the whole world. The world is on the edge of catastrophe."

"But It Will Be Too Late"

There is something still more chilling.

One visionary, seeing Our Lady so sad, said: "I know what makes you suffer. **It is because the day will come when we will wish we had listened** to what you have been telling us about loving, serving, and doing what you ask—**but it will be too late.**"

Only ten years later, "the river of blood, people killing people, bodies without heads" changed from prophecy to grim reality.

A nun in Rwanda wrote to me at the time, and said simply: "It is like the end of the world here." Another said: "Hell has swallowed us."

Balkans Also Warned in Advance

It is utterly amazing that we hear almost the very same words used to describe the horrors which occurred in the Balkans ten years after Our Lady is reported to have appeared in Medjugorje. The village itself, where Her message was heard, became an oasis of peace in a land of horror.

Fr. Franjo Radman, seeking relief for the afflicted in Bosnia, said:

"Everywhere I went, I brought with me a large photograph album of pictures of massacred children, of pregnant women whose babies had been ripped from them, of headless bodies, and the bloodied remains of old people who had deserved to live their last years in peace."

The Franciscan priest said that he felt "angry and inadequate" because there seemed no way to make such horrors real to anyone. He tells us: "*What I saw with my own eyes I could never have imagined, nor would I have believed these things if I had been told them by anybody else.*"

He mentioned entering a Muslim village over-run by Serbian forces and seeing a group of soldiers who appeared to be playing football. "I was wondering how they found time to play. But we discovered that the 'ball' was the head of a Muslim man." (Pg. 77 of *Marija*, by Heather Parsons, Robt. Andrews Press, 1993.)

Horror spread. Muslims began to fight Christians other than Serbs and with the same degree of atrocity. Murder had become contagious. Sides became blurred. *It was as though hell had suddenly become present on earth.*

Magnitude Difficult to Grasp

The scale of the killings in Rwanda and the Balkans, in ratio to the population of the United States, is so shocking as to seem unbelievable. In ratio to the population of the United States, in *each* of those countries the number killed would equal about *twenty five MILLION.* And most were killed in a matter of months. In both of these little countries, which had been warned by an anxious Heavenly Mother ten years in advance, when it came, it was sudden and overwhelming, like an earthquake or an avalanche from which they could not escape.

In addition to the dead in Bosnia (comparable in size to Ireland), there were almost three million homeless. Fr. Radman says people looked horrified when told of cases of cannibalism among the starving. He added: "It was too terrible to seem real. One man, a refugee, who by the time he was found and brought into Croatia for safety, had eaten all the fingers from one of his hands because, for twenty days beforehand, he had not eaten and his mind began to play tricks on him. He thought his fingers were food."

If this happened in Bosnia and Rwanda, what will happen in the rest of the world if the Akita update of the Fatima message is ignored?

Is It Too Late for Us?

It was at the very time Our Lady was reported to be giving messages in Rwanda and in the Balkans that the Bishop of Akita in Japan announced, on March 27, 1982, that Our Lady had come with a similar message for the entire world:

"Many men in this world afflict the Lord. If men do not repent and better themselves, the Father will inflict a terrible punishment **on all humanity.**"

As in Rwanda, we are told specifically what the punishment will be. Instead of a river of blood, it will be fire:

"It will be a punishment worse than the deluge, such as one will never have seen before. Fire will fall from the sky and will wipe out a great part of humanity... The survivors will find themselves so desolate that they will envy the dead."

If we ignore this message, the predicted punishment will now affect ALL humanity. And we have already had half a century to respond because, in the very words of the Bishop of Akita:

"It is the message of Fatima."

But we have largely ignored the part of the message of Fatima which states that the alternative to our response will be the annihilation of entire nations. Perhaps the reason it is ignored is precisely because it is so terrible, so unthinkable.

"Will Envy the Dead"

A TV news program (*Sixty Minutes*) about the tragedy in Rwanda showed a young Rwandan woman who was the only survivor of her family of eight. Her baby had been taken from her arms, grasped by the feet, and its head smashed against the wall beside her. She must have envied the other eight members of her family who were massacred in moments and would suffer no longer.

Multiply this by HALF A MILLION butchered men, women, and children in that small country. Add to this the thousands now jailed and waiting, one by one, to be sentenced and executed. Then, add the agony of all the members of their families. Truly, many must envy those for whom it was all over with the slash of a machete, the severing of a head.

To many, the most terrible part of the prophecy of Akita seems to be in those words: "*The survivors will find them-selves so desolate that they will envy the dead.*"

Indeed, this prophecy is so terrible that, even after nine years of inquiries, the local Bishop hesitated to publish it. He went to Rome for advice. Cardinal Ratzinger, custodian of the third secret of Fatima, reassured him that *what Our Lady said at Akita was substantially the same as what She revealed in the secret of Fatima.*

We people of the third millennium, who have ignored the message of Fatima, are warned that if the requests of Our Lady continue to be ignored, "several entire nations will be annihilated." It will be by fire, and it will affect *all humanity.*

We MUST Listen!

The catastrophes of Bosnia and Rwanda witness to the effect of ignoring God's warnings. It is too late for Bosnia. It is too late for Rwanda.

Will it be too late for us? Will we continue to ignore the alternative of fire engulfing the earth and wiping out "a great part of humanity?"

Yet *we know what we can do* to prevent it!

Indeed, Our Lady said at Akita that SO FAR, *She has been able to prevent it* because of the response of a few! She said:

"Pray very much the prayers of the Rosary. I alone **am able still to save you from the calamities which approach.** Those who place their confidence in me will be saved."

Many may take exception to the words that only Our Lady can save us. We will examine this in a moment. But in a word, although we deserve God's chastisement, as Blessed Jacinta of Fatima explained: "*In His Mercy, He has entrusted the peace of the world to Her.*"

We MUST listen to Her. We MUST do as She ASKS!

God has warned us by means of three great signs, un-precedented in history. In a recent (1993) interview, Sister Lucia has told us that "Fatima has just begun," and that *now* we must respond urgently to the basic requests of Fatima with *many* more First Saturday Communions of Reparation.

Three great signs from God emphasize its urgency.

Bishop John S. Ito explains that a wound appeared in the hand of a statue of Our Lady in his diocese of Akita, Japan. It bled profusely. The statue also "wept" human tears. Our Lady spoke of a terrible chastisement which Bishop Ito understands to be the third part of the secret of Fatima, which Our Lady revealed to the children after saying: "*Several entire nations will be annihilated.*"

"Our Lady said at Akita," Bishop Ito recalls, "*that SO FAR She has been able to hold back the chastisement.*" At an international seminar in Akita, in November, 1992, the Bishop said that the message given by Our Lady at Akita is of great urgency for the entire world.

CHAPTER TWO

At our peril, we ignore
THREE GREAT SIGNS FROM GOD

The first sign, *a miracle* at Fatima in 1917, was seen by tens of thousands of people from all levels of life. It had been *predicted at a specific time and place,* "so that all may believe."

If we *had* believed and done what was asked, Sister Lucia (the Fatima visionary) revealed in an interview in October of 1993: *"All of the wars which have since occurred could have been avoided."*

But after giving us this miraculous sign, unprecedented in history, God did not abandon us to the wave of atheism which subsequently swept over the world. He predicted another sign, which He called *"the GREAT sign,"* by which we would know that He was about to chastise the world. This took place on January 24-25, 1938.

The third and last sign was the dissolution of the Soviet Union.

The First Sign
Greatest Miracle in History

The miracle of the sun at Fatima in 1917 is to our time what the miracle of the Red Sea was in its time. It was also like the great miracle of fire in the time of Elias.

It had been raining heavily before the moment of the miracle. The vast hollow of Fatima was a sea of water and mud. Immediately after the miracle (which lasted about 12 minutes), the sea of water and mud had vanished as in the miracle of the red sea. But there was something even more extraordinary.

It seemed as though the sun itself crashed down upon the earth. The engulfing fire covered a radius of 32 miles! It was as in the time of Elias, when the prophet called fire from the sky so that *all would believe* that "God is God!" —and *the fire consumed not only the sacrifice offered by the prophet but the water in the trench around it.*

Thus, the miracle of Fatima had the elements of two of the greatest miracles in history. But what is more, the Fatima miracle happened at a PREDICTED TIME AND PLACE, *so that all may believe.*

How important must be this present hour!

Jesus said to towns, *which knew him well,* that if Sodom and Gomorrah had seen what they saw, they would have repented, and that in the day of judgment, it will go better for Sodom and Gomorrah.

How will it go for us in the day of judgment if we do not respond to this unprecedented sign given to our time, "*so that all may believe?*"

The Message

And what is it that we are asked to believe?

She foretold the rise of atheism in Russia, which would spread throughout the entire world, and that several entire nations will be annihilated. But Russia would be converted and an era of peace would be granted to mankind if her requests were heard.

Next, she told us WHAT to do in order to bring about a change in Russia and to prevent the annihilation of nations.

In 1973, on the anniversary of the great miracle of the sun at Fatima, Our Lady appeared in Akita, Japan, as Our Lady of All Nations, and said that now a chastisement worse than the deluge will come if the world does not respond.

The second sign was predicted by Our Lady of Fatima in the following words:

"When you will see the night illumined by an unknown light, you will know that it is the great sign that God is about the chastise the world."

The Second Sign

Fire

On the night of January 24-25, 1938, *almost one third of the world seemed to be on fire*. Fire engines streamed out of cities all over Europe to combat flames *which were not there*. From the Arctic in the north deep into Africa, from Bermuda in the west to the Ural Mountains in distant eastern parts of Russia, *millions thought it was the end of the world*. **It coincided with the outbreak of the second world war which ended in the use of atomic weapons.**

Radio communications between the U.S. and Europe stopped. Scientists, unable to explain it, described it as some form of Aurora Borealis. But the visionary of Fatima said: "I believe if scientists investigate they will find that it could not be an aurora. It is the great sign."

A scientist who had worked on the first atomic bomb confirmed, some thirty five years later, that the spectra of the light of 1938 *was the same as the false aurora created by an atomic explosion!*[1]

Still, God did not leave us to struggle blindly in the flood of evil. He gave still a third sign which, in some respects, seems even more grave: *the dissolution of the Soviet Union* **after which**, if we understand the words of Our Lady of Fatima well, **several entire nations may be annihilated if another request of Fatima** (First Saturday Communions of Reparation) **is not fulfilled.**

The LAST Sign

In various apparitions and locutions to the visionary of Fatima from 1929 to 1935, God referred to this last sign as the *saving* of Russia, the *conversion of Russia*, and "*the cessation of religious persecution in that country*," **which would take place after the consecration of Russia**

---

[1] See the book *State of Emergency*, and the motion picture film, of the same name, based on the true life experience of Dr. J. Rand McNally Jr., who made this discovery.

to the Immaculate Heart of Mary *by the Pope, in union with all the bishops of the world.*

All the bishops were notified by Pope John Paul II in their proper languages. They received copies of the acts of consecration of the world and of Russia, which had been made by Pope Pius XII. They were informed that these acts would be renewed at Fatima on May 13, 1982.

Unfortunately, it had not been made clear that the Pope wanted the bishops to JOIN with him in this act. So, the following year, a second letter went out to all the bishops of the world asking them *to join* with the Pope in *a collegial* act of consecration, which then took place in Rome in union with all the Bishops of the world, on May 13, 1984.[2]

Nine months later, the change in Russia astonished the U.S. Central Intelligence Agency. The complete dissolution of the Soviet Union followed within six years.

---

[2] Some questioned whether this consecration was made in the proper manner, because some bishops may not actually have joined with the Pope as they were asked, and because Russia was not explicitly mentioned in the act itself. But the entire document of the consecration of Russia, made by Pope Pius XII, had been sent *in its entirety* to all the bishops of the world, and they had been told that this was what was being renewed, in union with them. If some bishops did not comply, it would not have changed the fact that all were informed, all were asked, the intention to consecrate Russia had been made clear, and the vast majority of bishops complied. Subsequently, Sister Lucia said that Our Lord accepted this consecration. The change in Russia followed almost immediately.

CHAPTER THREE

"I WANT MY ENTIRE CHURCH TO KNOW"

When the visionary of Fatima asked Our Lord why He insisted that the consecration be made by all the Bishops of the world, He answered: *"Because I want MY ENTIRE CHURCH TO KNOW that this favor (the change in Russia) was obtained through the Immaculate Heart of My Mother."*

Atheism Spread from Russia

The first of the Fatima prophecies was that "error will spread from an atheist Russia throughout the entire world." But, if Our Lady's requests were heard, Russia would be "converted," which means turned around, changed.

One of the first signs of the dissolution of the Soviet Union was in the meeting of Gorbachev with the Pope (in which the Soviet premier said that the persecution of religion had been their greatest mistake). *The spread of militant atheism throughout the entire world, which had been funded by Russia, now ceased.*

Archbishop Nguyen Van Thuan, while stationed in Rome in 1998, said that while *previously, all religion was persecuted as part of the Marxist belief that all religion is harmful,* "those in power today (*even in Vietnam, still officially atheist and communist*) no longer hold to this rigid ideological opposition to religion."

But **Atheism remained** with its effect of worldwide immorality and materialism.

"I Want My Entire Church to Know"

The bloodless dissolution of the Soviet Union, which the Pope said can hardly be explained outside the context of the message of Fatima, is a sign from God, perhaps even more important than the sign of the miracle and the "great sign." It is for this present time of practical atheism.

For more than half a century, we had been expecting the change in Russia when enough persons had fulfilled the basic Fatima requests. *But, when it finally came, we seem to have forgotten the last of the prophecies given at Fatima:*

"Several entire nations will be annihilated... To prevent this I shall come back to ask for the consecration of Russia and the First Saturday Communions of Reparation."

When Our Lady returned to give *the details of the First Saturday devotion,* She asked that ALL THE BISHOPS OF THE WORLD join with the Pope in consecrating Russia to Her Immaculate Heart.

Pope John Paul II, in union with all the bishops of the world, makes the consecration to the Immaculate Heart of Mary in St. Peter's square. The statue was flown from Fatima for this solemn, historic event.

During the reign of five different Popes, time after time, the consecration was made, but always without notice to all the bishops of the world. And, as we said above, Our Lord explained that the consecration of Russia had to be made by *all the bishops of the world* because: "*I want My entire Church to know* that it is through the Immaculate Heart of My Mother that this favor (the change in Russia) is obtained, so that **it may extend this devotion later on,** and place this *devotion to Her Immaculate Heart alongside devotion to My Own Sacred Heart.*" (letter of Sr. Lucia, May 18, 1936).

Why Is This So Important?

Why was this devotion of such great importance that **God made the dissolution of the Soviet Union** *a sign for it to be promoted in the world?*

Was it because this would be a time when many were no longer going to confession (and confession is one of the conditions of the devotion)?

Or, was it because this would be a time of decreased devotion to the Eucharist, when *Communions of Reparation* would be needed?

We already had Communions of Reparation to the Sacred Heart on First Fridays. But now, God wanted also Communions of Reparation to the Immaculate Heart of Mary, which is wounded by the same sins. And this time, confession was to be made, and there were to be at least a quarter of an hour of meditation on the mysteries of the Rosary, together with its recitation, as aids to a worthy Communion of Reparation.

We will speak of this later. Let us continue to focus here on the almost incredible fact that God has given us *the dissolution of the Soviet Union as a sign that NOW this devotion MUST be promulgated and practiced.*

The Amazing Facts

Our Lord had told the Fatima visionary that this devotion was to be promulgated throughout the world after the change in Russia. This was revealed on May 29, 1930 in a letter to her confessor:

"**The Holy Father must then promise that upon ending this persecution** (the persecution of religion in Russia), **he will approve and recommend the practice of the reparatory devotion** (of the Five First Saturdays)."

As we said before and cannot repeat too often: On March 25, 1984, after communicating with all the bishops of the world, Pope John Paul II solemnly made the consecration at St. Peter's in Rome, and *it was followed almost immediately afterwards* (evident nine months later) by the change in Russia. Six years later came the complete dissolution of the entire Soviet Union.

It Took Sixty Seven Years!

The magnitude of this message from Heaven can be seen in the perspective of its total span of sixty seven years.

The "First Saturday Communions of Reparation" were first announced on July 13, 1917, after the prophecy of the annihilation of various nations. Details were given in 1927. Two years later, in 1930, Our Lord explained that they were to be promulgated especially after the cessation of religious persecution in Russia. Six years later, in 1936, He explained that He insisted on the collegial consecration so that "My entire Church will know," and will promulgate this devotion after the change in Russia. That finally occurred between 1984 and 1990.

NOW, after all those years, was the time!

But despite all this, and despite **the amazing sign given by God, "so all My Church will know,"** *the reparatory devotion has been largely ignored.*

Difficult to Understand Before Atom Bomb

It was difficult to understand in 1917 why Our Lady said at *that* time, after predicting *annihilation of several nations,* She would come to ask for the First Saturday Communions of Reparation *"to prevent this."*

It was difficult to understand because, at that time, atomic weapons did not exist. And at that time, we were being given just the basic requests of Fatima: offering up to God of our daily sacrifices, the Rosary, and consecration to the Immaculate Heart of Mary.

When asked in 1946 *what was necessary then* to respond to the message of Fatima, the visionary insisted on only those three things. When asked if the First Saturdays were not important, She said they were, but only in the context of those three basic requests.

She said the First Saturday devotion would renew us once a month and help us to do all three: extending the morning offering through the day with the help of prayer and consecration (the Rosary and the Scapular).

We Are In a New Phase

But, three years after the dissolution of the Soviet Union (Oct. 11, 1993), Sister Lucia delineated three phases of Fatima: the first was the apparitions; the second was to obtain the change in Russia; the third phase is to obtain the era of peace, while at the same time avoiding further use of atomic weapons.

She said that in the first phase, fulfillment of the basic requests *would have prevented all the wars which took place in that time.* In the second phase, **adding the First-Saturday devotion to the basic requests can prevent the annihilation of several entire nations**.

But let us keep always in mind that while we have been given a terrible warning of God's Justice, we have also been given a glorious, indeed almost unbelievable promise:

"Finally my Immaculate Heart will triumph. Russia will be converted and *an era of peace will be granted to mankind.*"

The Alternative

Many have presumed that those two promises would be fulfilled one after the other. Only lately have we begun to speak of an era of peace from a remnant of survivors. Indeed, the *threat of the annihilation of nations has become much greater after the dissolution of the Soviet Union,* after fifty years of balanced terror. When Pakistan was on the verge of an atomic attack on India in 1998, we were sharply reminded of the continuing and perhaps escalating danger.

But in His Omniscience and Mercy, God gave us three great signs:

1) The miracle of 1917, which was *fire coming down upon the earth,* causing all in an area of several miles to think it was the end of the world.

2) The great sign of 1938, which caused millions from Bermuda to the Urals, and from the Arctic into Africa, to think *the world was on fire.*

3) And finally, there came the bloodless change in Russia, immediately following the collegial consecration, which the Pope said seemed inexplicable, except in the context of Fatima. In that message, *the annihilation of several entire nations is the predicted alternative* to our failure to respond.

"The Third Day"

There have been three phases: the phase of promises and warnings, then fulfillment of the prophecies up to the collegial consecration, and now, the time *for the full message of the Two Hearts* (The Sacred Heart of Jesus and the Immaculate Heart of Mary) in the face of increasing danger of annihilation of nations.

During the interview with Cardinal Vidal on Oct. 11, 1993, the visionary of Fatima said: "*People expect things to happen immediately, within their own time frame. But Fatima is still in its third day. The triumph is an on going process.*"

Then, after repeating that Fatima is in its third day, she said: "*We are now in the post-consecration period. The first day was the apparition period. The second day was the post-apparition, the pre-consecration period. The Fatima week has not yet ended. I may not live to see the whole week... Fatima has just begun...*"

When asked whether Our Lady's requests were being fulfilled by the movement promoting the original basic pledge of Fatima together with emphasis on the First-Saturdays, she answered:

"I believe it does, because *this movement shows itself to be the fulfillment of what the Virgin spoke* to promote the Communion of Reparation, which is the means to combat atheism... *The Virgin is interested in everything* (*the entire pledge*) but particularly in the Communion of Reparation."[3]

The Aids

In a letter of Oct. 13, 1997, Pope John Paul II called the miracle of Fatima *one of the greatest signs of our times* because it brings us **face to face with the great alternative facing the world**, *the outcome of which,* said the Pope, "*depends upon our response.*"

The Fatima response is a "formula of holiness." We are asked *every day* to make the morning offering, with the help of a specific prayer and consecration to Her Immaculate Heart; and on First Saturdays—the Rosary with 15 minutes of meditation, confession, and Communion.

For just the first three requests, Our Lady promised the conversion of Russia. Now, for all four, She promises an "*era of peace for mankind!*"

And, "*everything*" She asks *is so little!* All four requests are so easy! Some twenty-five million around the world made the basic pledge. *Is it too much to hope that now they may renew it, and also make the First Saturdays?* Does such an effort for the final victory over the wave of evil, and the "era of peace for mankind" seem impossible?

So did the fall of the Berlin wall.

Sister Lucia said in the 1993 interview: "*God will help you and the Virgin will help you; may everything be accomplished!*"

She then added: "*For me,*" this apostolate of the Fatima pledge and the First Saturdays "*is a great reason for hope.*"

That hope brightened in 1999 when Mrs. Helen Bergkamp, of Wichita, Kansas, felt inspired to place, at the International Center of the Queen of the World in Fatima, a large statue of the Immaculate Heart with a recess beneath Her Heart in which to place people's names.

---

[3] At the time, the author played an important part in this "movement" (to which Sister Lucia refers) as editor of VOICE Magazine. Within four weeks of this interview, in which Sister Lucia also referred to the efforts of Satan to destroy it, Cardinal Vidal wrote to the author: "We hope that our partnership in the apostolate of the Two Hearts will remain forever."

"I was inspired by the example of St. John Vianney," she said, "who had a similar statue in which he placed the names of his parishioners. I felt this would offer an opportunity for parishioners of the world to brighten the new millennium with hope of renewed consecration to the maternal Immaculate Heart of Mary, with a promise to fulfill Her requests."

Thanks to digital technology, the recess in the heart of the statue can receive and hold millions of names.

Closeup of the heart of the statue (pictured on back cover), in which names will be placed on a computer disk. The prayer on the heart reads: "*Holy Mary Mother of the universe, pray for us. Hold us forever in the protection of your maternal heart until we are safe in paradise.*"

CHAPTER FOUR

DAY OF THE IMMACULATE HEART

Pope John Paul II said that Fatima "compels the Church." The first sign (the miracle of the sun) was so that "*all may believe.*" In the second, specifically called "The Great Sign," *a great part of the world appeared to be on fire...* "*God was about the punish the world.*"

As pointed out in the previous chapter, the reason for the third and most recent sign (*the cessation of religious persecution in Russia*) was **given by Our Lord Himself:** "That My entire Church will know it is through *the Immaculate Heart* of My Mother that this favor is obtained (i.e. the change in Russia) so that *afterwards* it may extend this devotion *and place it alongside devotion to My Own Sacred Heart.*"

This "third day of Fatima," which began at the end of the twentieth century, is *the day of the Immaculate Heart.*

But for millions *it is as though that day never dawned.* It is as though God's interventions to awaken the conscience of the world, with so many signs to obtain response from believers, were not even happening.

Other Signs

In his recent monumental book *The Fatima Prophecies*, Dr. Tom Petrisko likens Fatima to a wall, raised to prevent mankind from plunging forward to self-destruction. All the other signs and wonders are Divine posters on the wall crying out: "*Stop here!*"

Dr. Petrisko details dozens of credible Divine interventions emphasizing the message of Fatima—dozens of new posters on the wall.

Many of these are confirmed by miraculous signs, although some are too recent to have had full evaluation and approval by the Church. Two in particular (which took place in Amsterdam and Akita) have already been declared credible by Church authority. Those posters, crying STOP HERE!, seem almost as big as the wall itself.

At the conclusion of his more than four hundred page work, Dr. Petrisko makes the sage observation that, although God "said it all" at Fatima, in His great mercy, He has given more signs and messages because the three great signs of Fatima, and His message through the Immaculate Heart of Mary, have been so widely ignored.

Our Lady of All Nations

Two large and most compelling posters on the wall were placed there by OUR LADY OF ALL NATIONS. A wooden statue of Our Lady of All Nations in Akita, Japan, "came alive" to deliver an earth-shaking message released by the local Bishop in March, 1984. Miracles confirming the message included the instantaneous cure of the nun who received it and who had previously been incurably deaf. Some five hundred persons saw the statue shed human tears (confirmed by carefully controlled scientific analysis) one hundred and one separate times.

The image of Our Lady of All Nations originated from apparitions in Amsterdam, Holland, some forty years before, which subsequently received Church sanction. It is an image of Our Lady standing before the cross, Her hands extended downwards as on the miraculous medal.

This "poster" on the wall crying "Stop here!" has a new ring of urgency. When the bishop who approved the apparitions in Akita was asked: "What is the message?," he answered: *"It is the message of Fatima."*

At Fatima, Our Lady spoke of the annihilation of entire nations. At Akita, She speaks of a "chastisement worse than the deluge," which is "at hand."

Stop Here!

The wall built by Our Lady at Fatima in the name of God, confirmed by the "greatest, most colossal miracle in history," says: *"Men must cease offending God Who is already so much offended"* (the last words of Our Lady of Fatima before the miracle of the sun).

It says: *"Stop here!"*

She warned that, if we ignore this wall, beyond it we will meet a great catastrophe: *"several entire nations will be annihilated."*

Lest we should doubt that this is still to come if we do not respond, it was in 1984 (year of the collegial consecration of Russia to Her Immaculate Heart, followed soon after by the dissolution of the Soviet Union) that the Akita poster appeared on the wall: *"The chastisement is at hand... It will be worse than the deluge."*

The Lady of All Nations was merely repeating what She had said at Fatima. If the world does not heed these signs from God, *"much of humanity will be destroyed by fire."* And, She added the somewhat terrible words: "Those who survive will envy the dead" (as foreshadowed in the events in Rwanda, mentioned in our very first pages).

Instructions on the Wall

The wall God put in our path at Fatima to save mankind from plunging forth to self destruction is not only a wall which says: "Do not pass." *It is a wall on which is written, in bold letters, God's instructions for turning back.*

Pope John Paul II tells us that: *Fatima is one of the greatest signs of the times not because of the miracle but because it indicates the RESPONSE necessary for meeting the alternative now facing the world:* **"to save mankind from self-destruction."**

CHAPTER FIVE

WHY THE IMMACULATE HEART?

Perhaps one reason for the meager response to the miracle of the sun, to the Great Sign, to the challenge made by Jesus following the dissolution of the Soviet Union, is that many do not understand WHY God should have Our Lady say at Fatima that She came because: *"God wishes to establish in the world devotion to My Immaculate Heart."*

The leprous Syrian nobleman refused to bathe in the Jordan, at the command of the prophet Eliseus, because he could not understand. Were there not better rivers in his own country?

And are there not greater things we might do in this atomic age than take refuge in the Immaculate Heart of Mary?

But look at our leprosy. It is far more terrible than leprosy of the body. It is the leprosy of a turning away from God. And as we fail to cry out for His Mercy, we ourselves call down His Justice.

But as Our Lord revealed to Blessed Faustina, this is a time *of exceptional mercy.* Therefore, "He has entrusted the peace of the world to Her," expressed little Jacinta, youngest of the Fatima children. He had sent our Redeemer through Her. Now He wills that we bathe in the river of Her love and be delivered from our leprosy.

Our Lady said that the reason our Heavenly Mother and Queen was sent to mankind at Fatima is because *"only She can save them."*

Most writers substitute: "only She can *help*," because in an absolute sense only GOD can save. But the Portuguese words Our Lady spoke, exactly as Lucia recorded them, are: "*Porque so Ela lhes podera valer.*" This means *only She can save—or protect. (Documentos de Fatima,* edited by Father Antonio Martins, S.J., pg. 339.)

Why So Explicit?

Why did Our Lady use words which might cause us to hesitate to quote them for fear they might be considered "untheological," or be misunderstood?

Little Jacinta told us why. She said, as a matter of fact: "*God has entrusted the peace of the world to Her.*"

Again, we may ask *why.* The answer is *because this is God's Plan.* We *deserve* annihilation. He has given us **the Mother**—the Mother of the Savior, whom the Savior Himself gave us from the cross—**to save us from annihilation**.

And why does Our Lady emphasize this at the very time She predicts annihilation (almost apologetically, in the third person)? Why does She say that men must turn to Her, listen to Her?

Ah...therein we behold the mercy!

She Needs So Little!

She can ask *little things*, which She can offer up with the Passion of Her Son, from Her own Sorrowful and Immaculate Heart, and thereby blind Satan, and turn aside the just wrath of God.

She told the children over and over to say the Rosary. She even used the words: "You *must* say the Rosary."

And why? Because it is a little thing possible to children and adults, to young and old. *Yet it touches upon the mysteries of God* and causes Him to see us not in the black of our evil but *in the light of Her love*, in the blinding purity of Her Immaculate Heart.

And that is why She held the Scapular out of the sky at the climax of the miracle performed, "so that all may believe."

"*She wants all to wear it,*" said Lucia, "*it is the sign of consecration to Her Immaculate Heart.*" It is a cloak not only to protect us but to *show us before God as Her chil-*

dren, for whom She suffered with Jesus on Calvary. How could His Justice annihilate these children under Her mantle of love?

Oh, blessed words: "*Only SHE can save you!*" Oh, words of God's Mercy!—the Mercy Which cried from the Cross: "*Behold your mother!*" Let us never hesitate to use them and to shout them to the world: "Only SHE can save you!" Listen to Her! She can save you with *little, easy things.* God's Merciful plan has made this possible.

God's Plan

That giant "Akita poster" on the Fatima wall bears the title: 101. It was fixed there by 101 miracles of tears. The angel of Akita explained that the number 101 recalled Genesis 3:15. The circle represented God, with Eve to the left and Mary to the right. The first lost God's Grace. Through the second, God restored it. And now, by His Mercy, the Mother of all Nations, through whom Grace in Jesus was restored to man, comes to deliver our immoral age.

This age has been called the "sexual revolution." It should also be called revolution against God's law. And it seems universal. Even some within the Church reject *Humane Vitae.*

The antidote is the Immaculate Heart of Mary. It is the antidote of God's Love. Also, like going to bathe in the Jordan, it is a humble submission to God's plan.

To be consecrated to the Immaculate Heart of Mary is to acknowledge the great "101" plan of God. It is to affirm our belief that, *through Mary,* God became man to redeem us, and to be our Eucharist. It is to cry out to God that we acknowledge our sinfulness and turn to Him for conversion and mercy *in union with the flaming love of the Immaculate Heart of our Mother.*

Many, not understanding why God gives this condition to save this nuclear age, may ask: "Why should we be consecrated to the Immaculate Heart of Mary rather than directly to Jesus?"

This is no mystery to those who know and understand the plan given by God, when man first sinned. That plan, clearly stated in Genesis 3:15, is now reaching fulfillment.

"Between Your Seed and Her Seed"

The enmity between Satan and the new Eve is also between the seed of Satan "and Her seed." The way to victory is through Her Immaculate Heart. Becoming the Mother of Jesus, She became the Mother of grace in each of us. Experience confirms that the surest, *easiest way to be consecrated to the Heart of Jesus is to be consecrated to the Immaculate Heart of Mary.*

At Fatima, we are invited to immerse our hearts in Her Heart Immaculate in order that we may be wholly and completely with Jesus as She is. And in this third day of Fatima, Jesus Himself gives us this call. He has asked us, after the change in Russia, *"to place devotion to Her Immaculate Heart next to My Own Sacred Heart."*

Confirmed by the Magisterium

This is confirmed by the magisterium of the Church. Pope Pius XII made it a "command." Declaring that "in the doctrine and devotion of the Queen of the World, Our Lady of All Nations, lies the world's greatest hope," Pope Pius XII *mandated* (in his encyclical *Ad Caeli Reginam*) that each year on the feast of Our Lady's Queenship there be a renewal of *consecration to Her Immaculate Heart.*

Pope Paul VI repeated this call in *Signum Magnum*: "We exhort all the children of the Church to consecrate themselves again, *each one*, to the Immaculate Heart of the Mother of the Church, to submit more and more to the Divine Will in *living out* this very noble act of piety and, finally, to serve it piously as children, in accordance with the example of their Heavenly Queen."

John Paul II not only consecrated the world to the Immaculate Heart but, in many journeys, he made acts of consecration to Her Immaculate Heart of many individual nations. In his encyclical *Dives in Misericordia* (par. 15), he said that he sees, in consecration to the Immaculate Heart of Mary, "the most efficacious means of obtaining Divine Mercy upon the Church and upon all humanity."

We do not have to understand it. But, the more we respond, like the Syrian noble who went into the Jordan and was cured of his leprosy, the more we will understand God's plan, and the more (and the sooner) we will see His promise fulfilled.

Popes Have Shown the Way

In 1942, Pope Pius XII, in keeping with the message of Fatima, consecrated the world (with a special mention of Russia as "that land where the icon of Our Lady lies hidden, awaiting a better day") to the Immaculate Heart of Mary. In 1954, the same Pope made an explicit consecration of Russia to the Immaculate Heart.

Both of those consecrations to the Immaculate Heart were renewed by Pope Paul VI *in the Vatican Council,* immediately following promulgation of the major Council document *Lumen Gentium.*

The same two acts of consecration to the Immaculate Heart were renewed by Pope John Paul II, **in union with all the bishops of the world,** on March 25, 1984.

Each time the pontiffs made these universal acts of consecration to the Immaculate Heart of Mary, *they called for INDIVIDUAL consecration of persons, families, and nations* to the Immaculate Heart. And as we mentioned above, in journeys throughout the world, Pope John Paul II made specific acts of consecration to the Immaculate Heart of Mary, in many individual nations.

If the example and mandates of these Popes had been followed, might we not already have had not only a change in Russia but in the entire world?

Reason for Hope

While we ask if it might be too late to awaken those who have failed to respond to these mandates of the Popes, the year before he died, Pope Paul VI seemed to voice the same question in an interview with Jean Guitton.

Speaking of the signs of our times as the signs of the "last times," the Pope said, in the face of so much apostasy, he often pondered on the words of Our Lord: "When the Son of Man comes, will He find any faith in the world?"

But, let us rephrase the question "Too Late?" to: "Is it too late *to hope for a worldwide crusade* to obtain the needed response?"

If so far not enough persons have consecrated themselves to the Immaculate Heart of Mary in the sense of fulfilling the basic conditions for Her triumph, is it perhaps because they did not know? If not enough have responded to the signs and messages from God and the exhortations of the Popes, is there *anything* which can be done to inspire millions to respond *now?*

Something is happening at the ancient Castle of Fatima which is so simple that it may be the answer. In a world center of devotion to Our Lady of All Nations, the statue of the Immaculate Heart, mentioned at the end of Chapter Three, awaits the names of millions who may yet be moved to consecrate themselves and their families to the Immaculate Heart of Mary, before it is too late.

CHAPTER SIX

HOW LATE IS IT?

P resuming that it is not too late, how late is it?
If the world continues to ignore the wall and all its posters, if a new project for worldwide individual consecration to the Immaculate Heart of Mary should fail, will mankind go on to self destruction?

Certainly the time is short. Pope John Paul II said, in his book *Crossing the Threshold of Hope*: "As we near the millennium, it seems the words of Our Lady of Fatima are nearing their fulfillment."

In his Fatima letter of Oct. 13, 1997, acknowledging Fatima as one of the greatest signs of our time, the Pope said that it was great not so much because of the unprecedented miracle of Oct. 13, 1917 but because Our Lady came to give us THE SPECIFIC RESPONSE to meet the alternative of our time—to "save man from self destruction."

Certainly, when His Holiness wrote this near the end of 1997, he did not think it was too late.

Animated Poster on the Wall

A great event took place in Moscow shortly after the dissolution of the Soviet Union.

On the Russian feast of Our Lady of Victories, October 16, 1992, two giant jumbo jets, carrying almost a thousand pilgrims, flew over the Kremlin to bring to Russia the statue of Our Lady, known as the Pilgrim Virgin, which had set forth from Fatima for Russia in 1947.

Hundreds of others came from many other nations to join in this historic event, which took place on the very day of one of the major Marian feasts of the Orthodox Church and the day, just fifty years before, that St. Maximilian Kolbe had founded the Militia of the Immaculate, and prophesied: "One day, Our Lady's cavaliers will bring Her statue over the highest point of the Kremlin, into the heart of Moscow."

The Metropolitan of Moscow and the Roman Catholic chaplain of the pilgrimage *prayed together* before a miraculous copy of the Patroness of Russia, Our Lady of Kazan, in Moscow's Cathedral. It was the first time such an event had taken place since the schism between Moscow and Rome, almost a thousand years before.

When the Pilgrim Virgin was crowned the next day in Red Square, *Our Lady was seen over the square crowned as Queen.* Rays of light streamed *from Her Immaculate Heart* into the square and exploded back in all directions, *as though to illuminate the world.* (For details see the book *Finally Russia,* 101 Foundation, 1993, 186pp.)

The Pilgrim Virgin had traveled through many nations for fifty years in an aura of miracles like an animated poster on the wall of Fatima. It was as though Our Lady Herself went all over the world to evoke RESPONSE to the conditions being given to us by God to end corruption of nations and to avoid their destruction.

"I crowned Her Queen of the World at Fatima," said Pope Pius XII, "and the following year, She set forth as the Pilgrim Virgin, *as though to claim Her dominion.* The favors She performs along the way are such that we can hardly believe what we are seeing with our eyes."

We had ignored so many posters on the wall. The Pope said it was "as though Our Lady Herself went forth to claim Her dominion"—to draw us to Her Immaculate Heart—to hear Her requests. Many described the wonders of the Pilgrim Virgin as those of "a loving, *anxious* Mother."

Now at the Fatima Castle

For more than half a century, the cry and the favors of Our Mother, *inviting us in the presence of the Pilgrim Virgin to take refuge in Her Immaculate Heart,* echoed through most of the world.

Now this same Pilgrim Virgin is going to have a permanent home at a world center of the Queen of the World at the

Fatima Castle as part of the project mentioned at the end of the last chapter: a final effort for worldwide response.

When now we ask the question "TOO LATE?," are we not in effect asking if *it is still possible* that, in addition to the few who have responded in the past, there may be a way to obtain a sufficient number to respond now, in time to turn mankind from its path to self-destruction?

We must presume that *God has not given us so many great signs in vain.* We must presume that, if we do our part, God will do still more wonderful things, such as a universal illumination of men's consciences.

The Fatima week has just begun. *The end of the week will be "an era of peace for mankind."*

Finally ... Russia!

CHAPTER SEVEN

A NEW OPPORTUNITY

S *tatues from nations all over the world are enshrined in the Castle at Fatima to create an international* **Center of the Queen of the World.** In a special place is a large statue of the Immaculate Heart with a recess beneath the heart to receive as many as a hundred million names on computer disc.

Here, names from all nations can be gathered "in Our Lady's Immaculate Heart" to honor Her as the Lady of All Nations, and in pledge of fulfilling Her conditions for world peace.

A similar, very simple plan fifty years ago, when the "Blue Army" offered to bury in the ground of Fatima the names of all who would pledge to fulfill the basic requests of Our Lady, led more than twenty-five million around the world to respond.

The "battle cry" then was for the conversion of Russia.

Now the challenge is different, and perhaps even more urgent. And before saying more about the Queen of the World project at the Fatima Castle, let us take a look at the most recent prophecies and what might now trigger a world catastrophe.

But first a warning:

Beware of Setting a Time

While it is proper that we anticipate what might trigger catastrophe in our world, we must not divert our attention from what Pope John Paul II said so succinctly on Oct. 13, 1997: *What is most important about Fatima is that it provides* **the specific response** *needed to turn mankind* *back from the path to self-destruction.* Everything else is peripheral.

But at this crucial moment, it is proper for us to evaluate our position. Some voices have specified dates. Some may lead us to believe that catastrophic events are to be expected almost from day to day.

During my lifetime, which spans most of the twentieth century, one of my major surprises has been, over and over, that predicted events happened much later than expected. One example of this has a double value.

"Do You Not Believe?"

In the pre-consecration period, the major response to the message of Fatima was made by the Blue Army, also known as the World Apostolate of Fatima. As the reader already knows, it was joined by some twenty-five million in over 100 countries.

Much of the success was due to the strong support of the Pope through the most powerful Cardinal of the fifties, His Eminence Eugene Cardinal Tisserant. But there was unexpected opposition from other quarters in Rome.

When the president of the Blue Army in Italy suddenly died, the Bishop of Fatima sent me to Rome to help select a successor. I then learned the name of the person high in one of the congregations who was behind much of the opposition. I decided to expose him in a book I was writing.

Shortly afterwards, I met with a holy priest in Rome who had the power of reading souls. At the very beginning of our meeting, he said: "About that high personage you are planning to expose, do not do it." I was amazed that God had revealed my thoughts to him.

On the wall above where we were seated was a picture of the Immaculate Heart of Mary. Pointing to the picture, he said severely: "Don't you believe that She is truly Queen? Do you not know that if it were God's Will, that man would be removed?" As he spoke those last words, he swept the air abruptly with his arm, as though it were a sharp scythe.

The holy priest had made me realize that even though our apostolate was being harmed, it was wrong to harm a reputation. Such things were to be left to God.

Years passed in which I kept silent, expecting to hear of the death of this influential person who was causing us so much harm. But it was only after more than THIRTY years that he was removed (and not by death but in public disgrace for deviations from the magisterium).

So, often what was expected to happen in months, or in a year, took decades. We should not be surprised that Sister Lucia said: "The Fatima week has just begun."

We should not be surprised if the end of the Fatima "week" did not come until well into the new millennium.

Opposition from Within

In the case of the example just given, the person in question was the right hand of the Cardinal Prefect of a most influential congregation, with input into much of the rest of the Roman curia, since the Cardinals often serve on several different boards. He was not just against the apostolate of Fatima. He was against the very idea of stressing consecration to the Immaculate Heart of Mary. He said in the one interview I had with him: "The Rosary is no longer relevant."

In a book of memoirs (*Dear Bishop,* AMI Press, 340pp), which I wrote at the request of my bishop, I gave some brief details of the opposition encountered in Rome, when we were asking the participation of Pope Paul VI in a world-wide renewal of consecration to Our Lady. This renewal was to take place in some fifty countries, on the occasion of the fiftieth anniversary of the coronation of Our Lady at Fatima as Queen of the World. The Pope was willing, but there seemed a veritable wall of opposition around him. We finally succeeded only when the bishops from all those countries joined in a petition.

This raises two questions:

1) How could that person who so opposed this effort reach so high a position and have so much influence in the Church?

2) Why did God permit it?

Was it perhaps because the opposition made the final result all the more powerful because:

a) all those bishops around the world requested the Pope's participation;

b) because despite all the opposition, the Pope participated both by radio and television?

Whatever the reason, opposition to proclaiming the Queenship of Mary, and that She is our Mediatrix and Advocate, is bewildering to much of the laity. I will never forget the moment Pope Paul VI said to me, speaking about that worldwide affirmation of Our Lady's Queenship: "It is very difficult."

I was wondering how it would be difficult for the Pope, the supreme head of the Church, to take so small an action. Then, having turned to leave, the Pope suddenly turned back and said almost sadly: "Pray for me."

The year before he died, he told Jean Guitton (*The Secret Paul VI*, pg. 152) that he found himself "often repeating to myself those obscure words of Our Lord: 'When the Son of man returns, will He still find faith on the earth?'" He was perhaps deeply wounded at the number who rejected *Humanae Vitae*, upon which he had prayed and labored more than six years. He told Guitton that what he found most strange was not so much that false doctrine appears now in so many books but that the bishops do not clearly denounce them.

"I sometimes read the Gospel of the end times," the Pope said, "and I attest that some signs of these times are emerging... What strikes me is that within Catholicism there seems sometimes to predominate a non-Catholic way of thinking. And it can happen that this non-Catholic thought within Catholicism may become stronger. It is necessary that a small flock subsist, no matter how small it may be."

Those words seem to say "too late." But in the face of the opposition, John Paul II countered with the example of a total consecration to Our Lady—with *Vertitatis Splendor*, and the marvelous new Catechism.

Could the opposition be a part of the purification? Could it be part of what is necessary for the final triumph of the Church under the mantle of the Mother of the Church?

The former bishop of Garabandal, when he retired, said that he had come to believe in the Garabandal events and messages, but one thing bothered him: That Our Lady had said Cardinals would be against Cardinals and Bishops against

Bishops. Being a good bishop himself, he could not think of opposition of other bishops.

This is one of the problems of our time. The world's top expert on Fatima, the Rev. Joachim Alonso, believed this to be part of the third secret of Fatima.

It should not surprise us. It should not discourage us. *Instead, it should cause us to pay close attention to one of the posters on the wall, which was put there by Our Lady of All Nations, in great, bold letters: ENCYCLICALS.*

In Amsterdam, She said: "Christianity, do you know the great danger you are in? There is a spirit out to undermine you. But the victory is Ours." Then, as the word ENCYCLICALS appeared in large letters, She said: "*Do you realize how powerful is this force? Know well your time has come. This is our time.*" (Note: These words of Our Lady of All Nations were one of the inspirations of my recent book *Now The Woman Shall Conquer,* with special reference to the encyclicals *Ad Caeli Reginam* and *Signum Magnum.*)

Vision of St. John Bosco

Despite all the reason for concern, many before the new millennium were encouraged by the prophetic vision of St. John Bosco.

It had five elements:

1) There would be a victory before the third millennium "greater than the victory of Lepanto;"

2) The bark of Peter would be storm tossed, sometimes even seeming to disappear beneath the waves;

3) The Pope would be at the helm through the storm;

4) The Pope would guide the bark between two pillars of Our Lady and the Eucharist;

5) When the bark was tied to the pillars, it would be secure.

The victory "greater than Lepanto" took place after the collegial consecration of Russia in 1984. The Soviet Union was dissolved. The cold war was over. Militant atheism financed by international Communism from Russia ceased. It happened so suddenly, so unexpectedly and without bloodshed, that the Pope said it could hardly be explained other than in the context of Fatima.

Three other important observations should be made:

1) Our Lady appeared to St. John Bosco as *Queen*, crowned and sceptered, Her Divine Son in Her lap with crown and orb;

2) The victory of Lepanto was the turning point in the possible taking over of Europe *by Islam*;

3) Pope St. Pius V, who had united the Church in a Rosary crusade in the face of the great danger, declared that it was *Our Lady who had obtained the victory.* He thereupon named the day of the victory, Oct. 7, the Feast of Our Lady of Victories, later called the *Feast of Our Lady of the Rosary.*

It would be useful if the reader could keep all these aspects of the vision and prophecy of St. John Bosco in mind. They are extremely relevant not only to what has happened in the twentieth century but what will happen in the twenty-first.

Within the twentieth century, as the saint prophesied, we have seen a victory greater than Lepanto. And it was through Our Lady of the Rosary.

Storm is Not Over

But the storm is not over. The bark of Peter has not yet become fastened to the pillars. How many of us, even nations, may perish before the storm ends?

The battle of Lepanto, by the power of the Rosary, saved Europe from Islam. Now Islam is the most rapidly growing religion in the western world. It is predicted that Europe will become Islamic before the end of the 21st century. Some Islamic nations have nuclear missiles. Terrorists will have them.

What is happening at the Fatima Castle bears a special relationship to Islam.

CHAPTER EIGHT

RISING FROM THE EAST

The Blue Army stood for forty years before the Fatima wall crying out to the world for response to Our Lady's requests. It was a cry made shrill by the nuclear balance of terror.

As this battle cry died away, Our Lady reminded us at Akita, in a flood of miraculous tears, that there is still, looming beyond the wall, an ever increasing threat that "several entire nations will be annihilated." The Pope goes so far as to say that the need to respond to Our Lady's requests is "more urgent than before."

Her warning to Rwanda was not heard. Catastrophe followed ten years later. Our Lady is reported to have appeared in the former Yugoslavia as Our Lady of Peace, asking for conversion, prayer, fasting.

Just ten years later, even though the village where the message was accepted remained in peace, most of the Balkans were bathed in fratricidal blood in what became largely a Muslim-Christian conflict.

What might now trigger tragedy for the world in general? There are already enough nuclear devices to destroy all the nations of the world over and over. *But what might trigger their use?*

What I will now venture to say bears an unusual relation to Fatima.

Confrontation with Islam

Distracted by the impeachment of the U. S. President at the end of the twentieth century for gross immorality and lying under oath, immersed in consumerism, few Americans and even few Europeans were aware of an ever growing danger: the danger of nuclear terrorism.

The U.S. had made attacks on four Islamic countries: Libya, Afghanistan, Sudan, and Iraq (formerly the center of the Islamic empire). The Pope, aware of the danger, opposed the military strikes on Islamic nations.

But many in the major consumer nations ignored that this military action was hardening hatred in the hearts of hundreds of thousands of Muslims.

Islam is the not only the fastest growing religion in the world (already surpassing one billion), but is already a major power. An Arab oil embargo alone could virtually paralyze the major consumer nations. And almost all Islamic nations consider the major consumer nations to be evil. Many Muslims are ready to give their own lives to destroy the perceived enemies of Islam, evil before Allah. (And can we deny the extent of evil in the consumer nations?)

An Islamic Battle Cry

On Saturday, Jan. 30, 1999, members of the Iranian parliament chanted *"Death to America" as they extended a multi-million dollar fund to combat the United States.* Deputy speaker Hassan Rowhani, who chaired the session, said it was in response to U.S. military buildup in the Gulf. But the Islamic government had voted repeatedly for the same fund in previous years. Now the millions were voted again by the majority. And the battle cry was: *Death to America!*

In the past few years, we have seen an escalation of blood soaked Muslim violence in former Yugoslavia, Lebanon, Yemen, the Sudan, and Timor, to mention a few places in the world where the killing verges on genocide, while the average person in the major consumer nations seems hardly to care.

But what would be our attitude if the Muslim bombing of the World Trade Center had been with a nuclear device?

Bombs the size of a large suitcase could now destroy an entire city. And the materials have become increasingly available. Since the dissolution of the Soviet Union, smugglers of components of atomic bombs from Russia have been intercepted. Some of these components had been taken to Germany to be sold. *No one knows how many were not intercepted.* But we do know that part of Russia's stockpile of atomic weapon components is missing.

Is it too late to do anything about it? Is there anything we CAN do?

The answer (perhaps the ONLY answer) is Fatima.

What Is Islam?

"It is written in the Koran," according to Hasan al Banna, the founder of the Muslim Brotherhood, "Allah is our leader. The Koran is our Constitution. Holy War is our life. Death on the road of Allah is our supreme desire."

In 1571, Islam suffered a humiliating defeat at the hands of the Christians in the battle of Lepanto. Islam was in decline from that time until the recent rise of world dependency on oil. Now the lands of Mohammed are a growing center of great power.

Mohammed's public life passed between Mecca and Medina, where he organized his community in 622. His troops had taken the city in 630 and he had transformed the great cube of stone, La Kaaba, which represented more than three hundred and sixty deities, to his monotheistic doctrine. It became the holy site.

Despite divisions which arose after the death of Mohammed, the cult spread rapidly. In 636, Palestine and Syria were conquered, followed by Iraq in 638 and Egypt in 640. Two main divisions of Islam concerned right of succession: Sunnites and Shiites. The latter (strongest in Iran) hold that the only legitimate rulers of Islam are the blood descendants of Mohammed, *through his daughter Fatima.*

Destined to Rule the World

Mussulman domination spread from the Atlantic to the far East, including Portugal and Spain (dominated for seven hundred years), and the South of France as far as Poitiers, where they were stopped by Charles Martel. They ruled all the southern part of the former Soviet Union as far east as Chinese Turkestan.

Islam believes it is destined to rule the world. In the mosques of the Middle East, several of the present imams have predicted *that Europe will become predominantly Muslim in the 21st century.* Indeed, Islam is already the fastest growing religion in England. Two of the most dominant new religious buildings in Lisbon and Rome are Mosques.

To understand the phenomenal growth of Islam, one should know that a Jew or a Christian can convert to Islam, but not vice versa. Islam does not tolerate other religions. During the Gulf war, the chaplains of the American troops could not be called clergymen. They had to be labeled "psychologists."

A valuable book on this subject is *Les Confessions d'un Arabe Catholique.* It is a series of interviews with Bishop Abou Mokh of Damascus who, in 1967, was named to the Islam section of the Vatican Secretariat for non-Christians. (Interviews by Dr. Joelle Chabert, geologist and theologian, and by Rev. François Mourvillier, theologian. 255 pp, published by Centurion, 22 Cours Albert, 75008 Paris.)

"Today the Muslim world is a powerful world," says the Bishop. He sees the developments in Israel and attacks on Iraq as increasing Muslim hatred for the United States. He sees at once the *difficulty* and *the urgency* of this problem increasing throughout the world.

Any Solution Seems Impossible

There is one great difference between the threat from China of nuclear destruction of consumer nations and the threat from terrorists. China, like other nations, is subject to the balance of terror.

But *missiles and bombs are of no avail against terrorists.* And the more one studies the increasing threat, the more there appears to be no solution.

Muslims lived side by side with Christians under Tito for more than a generation. But massacres followed. And what could outside powers do to end the bloodshed in Algiers, Yemen, Timor, and Sudan? All the power of Russia proved inadequate in Afghanistan. Use of atomic weapons in such conflicts is unthinkable. Meanwhile the problem escalates.

In a pastoral letter of June 3, 1990, the Latin Patriarch of Jerusalem spoke of "hardening of the hearts of children ...radicalization of the position of adults." The pastoral pointed out what Judaism, Christianity and Islam have in common: "The value of the human person created in the image of God; the Justice of God and His Pardon; the traditional eastern values of welcoming the stranger, hospitality, generosity." The pastoral expressed hope in unity which seemed to develop among Christian and Muslim Arabs in their struggle for Palestinian identity.

Nine years later, that hope proved vain. In a passionate appeal on the eve of the last year of the twentieth century (Dec. 1999), the Auxiliary Bishop of the Jerusalem Patriarchate, Msgr. Kamal-Hanna Bathish, called for a "trialogue between Jews, Christians and Moslems." He said: "Must we await the year 2000 for the new millennium to start the trialogue? *I am sure it will be too late since it is already late!*" (*Inside the Vatican*, Jan. 1999, xvi.)

Mohammedans do not permit representations of the human figure. An extraordinary exception is the portrayal of the hand of the most glorious woman of Islam: *Fatima*, the daughter of Mohammed.

Chapter Nine

THE ANSWER

On August 13, 1917, two priests disguised in civilian clothes were in the crowd gathered at Fatima to see "what would happen."

A globe of light (which preceded all the apparitions) appeared in the eastern sky coming swiftly towards them. One priest exclaimed to the other: "Do you see that globe of light!? What do you think it is?"

In a voice tinged with awe the other answered: "I think it is the chariot of the Queen of Heaven."

The globe came from above a Castle, a few miles to the east of Fatima, which dated from the time of the Romans, and had been the center of government in the area of Fatima for almost 2,000 years.

Significance of the Name

Pope Paul VI called it "the Castle of the Queen of the World." Its official name is *Ourem*, from a Moorish princess whose Christian name was Oureana (after a saint little known today), and whose Islamic name was Fatima. She was buried on the hill opposite the Castle, thus giving that place, where Our Lady appeared in 1917, the name *Fatima*.

For more than a thousand years (from the time of the expulsion of the Moors in 1157), the Castle, and the place opposite where Our Lady appeared in our time as the Queen of the World, were linked by the Muslim and Christian names of a woman who might otherwise long have been forgotten in the pages of history.

At this Castle, there has now been established a possible catalyst for consecration to the Immaculate Heart of Mary, from nations all over the world, to obtain that great promise of Fatima: "*an era of peace for mankind.*"

Fatima, the Daughter of Mohammed, the Key?

The fact that God chose to give the world this promise at Fatima (the only place in all Europe which bears the name "Fatima") recalls that Mohammed said of his daughter Fatima: "**She has the highest place in Heaven after the Virgin Mary.**"

Those words are in the Koran, the Mohammedan holy book.

Since Islam teaches that the dignity of a woman depends on her relationship to a man, it follows that since the daughter of the founder of Islam has the highest place in Heaven *after Our Lady*, Her Son Jesus must have the highest place in Heaven.

"I do not ask why Our Lady appeared in Portugal, a land dedicated to Her," said Archbishop Fulton Sheen, "*but why did She choose that remote spot named Fatima, the only place in all Europe bearing that name?*"

Answering his own question, the famous Archbishop said he believed it was because Our Lady came not only for the conversion of Russia (which would ultimately mean all the Communist world) *but also for unity with Islam.*

Confirmed by Prince Pahlavi

"It is written in the Koran," as we previously quoted Hasan al Banna, the founder of the Muslim Brotherhood: "Allah is our leader. The Koran is our Constitution. Holy War is our life. Death on the road of Allah is our supreme desire."

Now, at the very time of today's rising power of Islam, Our Lady of the Rosary has appeared *at Fatima* promising "an era of peace for mankind." And to the amazement of his Muslim brothers, Prince Ali Pahlavi, who was in line of succession to the Shah of Iran, and *a descendant of Mohammed through his daughter Fatima*, wrote a book, *La Fille d'Imran,* in which he says:"Mary can bring Christianity and Islam together. I was myself a bit surprised about Mary's role while meditating on the Koran," the Prince said, "because in the Koran, *Mary as a virgin is comparable to Mohammed.*"

44

I do not hesitate to say that when I learned of this book, written by the successor to the Peacock Throne of Iran (where Fatima, the daughter of Mohammed, is buried in one of the holiest mosques of Islam) I felt that Our Lady of Fatima, *by that one act, had already begun the process.*

The more we discover, like Prince Ali Pahlavi, the more amazed we are.

Three statements in the Koran correspond to some extent to three of the five reasons given by Our Lord for reparation to the Immaculate Heart of Mary on five First Saturdays! The Koran says:

1) Mary is the Mother of Christ, with the highest place of any woman in Heaven;

2) She is ever virgin;

3) She is sinless, immaculate.

Castle of the Queen of the World

At the beginning of this chapter, we mentioned that the Castle of Fatima was given the Christian name of the Princess Fatima. For over a thousand years before being named after Fatima/Oureana, the Castle had been called "the Unconquerable."

How can one explain that the name of so important a fortress (which played a major role in Portuguese history) should have been renamed after this remote woman? Why should it not have been named for the first king who conquered it from the Moors? Or from the first Christian Count? And why is that same Castle now an international center of the Queen of the World for a worldwide response to the message of Fatima?

Cogent Reasons

The Castle was chosen to be an international center for consecration to Our Lady as Queen of the World because it *is* the Castle of the place where the Pope crowned and proclaimed Her to be *Queen of the World*. When passing the castle on his visit to Fatima in 1967, Pope Paul VI impulsively exclaimed: "The Castle of the Queen of the World."

Pope Pius XII named Our Lady of Fatima Queen of the WORLD because, at Fatima, She promised an era of peace "*to all mankind*." And after the conversion of the Communist world, *the key to that peace is rapprochement with the more than one billion Muslims* who teach that all who believe in the one True God must love one another.

Prince Ali Pahlavi, unless he already knows, would perhaps be greatly surprised to know that in the person and names of one Muslim Princess, Fatima/Oureana, may lie not only the hope he expressed of Christianity and Islam coming together but *hope of an "era of peace for mankind."*

Pope John Paul II referred to Fatima as the "Marian Capital of the World" not because Fatima is the greatest Marian Shrine in the world (several other Shrines are as great in size and numbers of pilgrims) but because *here an era of peace was promised for all mankind.* Here, two thousand years of history, the names Fatima/Oureana, the reason of the names, and the titles given to Fatima by the Popes, blend into a sign of hope.

Historic Place of Authority

Indeed, one does not fully understand Fatima without knowing the extraordinary history of this castle.

After being Muslim, Ourem became a court in which most of the languages of Europe were spoken. Its insignia became the Eagle of Savoy, long before nations like Poland and Russia, with that same escutcheon, were kingdoms. On the gate of this castle is still to be seen the coat of arms, which links dynasties from the Muslims to the day when a king of Portugal, in 1646, laid his crown at the foot of a statue of the Immaculate Conception and proclaimed Her Sovereign of the realm, vowing that never again would a Portuguese monarch wear the crown.

At the gate of the Castle, one can see the stone plaque placed there by command of the king, in 1646, proclaiming Mary Immaculate its Queen. And *from that gate one sees, piercing the sky on the opposite hill, the tower of the Basilica of Fatima, where the Pope crowned Her Queen of the World.*

A principal trustee of the Castle Foundation is Lord Duarte, who would be king of Portugal today if the monarchy were restored. He is the direct descendant of the king who, in 1646, placed his crown at the base of the statue of the Immaculate Conception and proclaimed Her Queen of Portugal. His royal highness is deeply and personally involved in *making this memorial to the Queen of the World a vehicle for a worldwide response, once and for all, to the conditions set forth by Her at Fatima for the triumph of Her Heart— for the "era of peace for mankind."*

Americans Played Major Role

Three Americans have played a major role in this project. One donated the original land and buildings. Two others, by the Providence of God, had already begun, years before, to make collections of images of Our Lady from all nations.

Armand J. Williamson had inaugurated a Marian Museum in New York. Mrs. Helen Bergkamp from Wichita, Kansas, had had a similar inspiration.

"During all these years I relied on Our Lady to guide us," says Mr. Williamson, "and when we learned of the development of the international memorial at the Fatima Castle, a center for worldwide response to Her conditions for world peace, Mrs. Bergkamp and I both knew at once in our hearts that this was the reason Our Lady had inspired us to gather Her images from all parts of the world."

Mrs. Bergkamp, as we have already mentioned, felt inspired to have a life sized image made of Our Lady of Fatima with a recess beneath Her Immaculate Heart, in which millions of names (on computer discs) could be stored.

In a special chapel at the entrance to the Castle, this image will receive the names of all those who join in this worldwide renewal of consecration to Her Immaculate Heart and pledge to fulfill Her conditions for conversion and world peace.

Greatest Miracle in History

Perhaps an entire book would be needed to explore adequately all the reasons why the Fatima Castle may be considered the ideal place in all the world for this perpetual memorial to Our Lady as Queen of the World. My recent book, *The Day I Didn't Die,* has two entire chapters on this subject. (See list at the end of this book.)

Over this Castle was seen what theologian/scientist Fr. Pio Sciatizzi, S.J., called "The greatest, most colossal miracle in history."

It was called the "miracle of the sun," but perhaps if the atom bomb had existed at that time, the fireball (which seemed about to engulf and consume the tens of thousands who saw it in the nearby Cova) would have been seen as a sign of the atom bomb.

God has willed today to emphasize the role of Our Lady as a powerful and conquering Queen. As Pius XII said in his encyclical *Signum Magnum,* She is the Woman *clothed with the Sun*, the Woman of the Apocalypse. She is *The Lady of All Nations* who *once*, that is, *in the past*, was simply known as Mary—Mary the Maid of Nazareth; Mary hidden in Scripture; Mary at the foot of the Cross, *now empowered to obtain an era of peace for mankind.*

CHAPTER TEN

WONDERFUL SIGN OF HOPE

At the moment of the inauguration of the Queen of the World Center at the Castle on August 22, 1996, the crowd, including some one hundred from the US, saw a miracle.

Tens of thousands saw the miracle of the sun in 1917. This was different. There were not so many witnesses and no fire plunged from the sky. But the witnesses were many, and worthy of belief.

I was 82 years old at the time and I affirm it was one of the three truly extraordinary experiences of my entire life. It is doubtful if any of the witnesses will ever be the same. One man who had been a nominal Catholic began going to Church every day and saying two to four rosaries daily.

"When I tell people I witnessed a miracle," says Ashley Puglia, of Springfield, Ill., "there are widely different reactions. Some react with disbelief: 'You must all have been hypnotized.' Some nod their heads as if they wanted to believe but knew better. Nevertheless, on August 22, 1996, feast of the Queenship of Mary, at the Castle of Ourem in Portugal, I saw a miracle."

One witness after the other says the same. Dr. Rosalie Turton, founder and President of the 101 Foundation, says:

"Sky and sun shimmered as though covered with silver dust. The sun itself turned blue. I have seen the so called 'miracle of the sun' many times before, particularly in Medjugorje, but this was the first time I ever saw it like this."

A family of three (Charles and Janet Papst and their teenage son) described "wide bands of rays through the clouds over the countryside of Fatima (opposite the Castle). Mary was standing at the right side of the Fatima Basilica with Her arms extended downward (as in the image of Our Lady of All Nations)."

"Never in my life have I ever experienced anything more beautiful," said Mrs. Armantine Keller, of Memphis, Tennessee.

Gena Ehrhardt, of Gallaudet University in Washington, DC, said that when she saw Our Lady in the sky with Her arms extended downwards, "I wanted to kneel. I was in amazement and awe. I felt that Our Lady had come to receive Her crown."

All of these testimonies are from written depositions and more will be found in my book *The Day I Didn't Die.* As one of the witnesses said: "This marvel overwhelmed us with the realization that it is God's Will that Our Lady shine before the world as the Queen of Peace." Another said: "*It is a sign of hope that from this center honoring the Queen of the World, the call to respond to Her Fatima message will finally be heard.*"

These wonders, attributed *only to God,* highlight the wall of Fatima, and seem to say: "*It is not too late!*"

When instituting the Feast of Her Queenship in 1954, Pope Pius XII said: "In this doctrine and devotion (of Our Lady's Queenship) *lies the world's greatest hope.*"

That hope has now taken form. It is at the Fatima Castle where images of Our Lady from all nations are being gathered, and where a statue of Her Immaculate Heart waits to receive the names of all those, from all the nations of the world, who will respond to Her call and to Her promise: "There will be an era of peace for mankind."

New Battle Cry

The pre-consecration battle cry (before 1984) was: "Russia will be converted." If we look at all the posters on the wall, what will be the Battle Cry now?

"Several entire nations will be annihilated," one poster says. But we cannot use a battle cry of doom. The word

PEACE is there, over and over. But only people at war are motivated by a promise of peace. The words PRAYER AND PENANCE loom large. But will that motivate the world to respond?

We may find the answer in the message of Our Lady of All Nations, a message finally sanctioned by the Church just before the new millennium.

As we have so often repeated, the Pope said that "in this doctrine and devotion of Mary's Queenship lies the world's greatest hope." And in doing so (in the 1954 encyclical), he related the doctrine of Mary's Queenship to Her dignity of Co-Redemptrix and Mediatrix. She is Queen not only by right, as the Mother of the King of Kings, but also by conquest— with Him on Calvary. And Our Lady of All nations said that when those attributes are defined, Her triumph will come.

Some five million have already signed petitions for their definition. Their Battle Cry seems to be "To obtain Our Lady's victory!"

What the Battle Cry Cannot Be

Battle cries will be inspired by future events themselves. But even in the event of nuclear terrorism in an European or American city, a new Battle Cry could never be "For the conversion of Islam." It could be only to bring Islam and us *together*.

We were much criticized in the past for using those words of Our Lady *"for the conversion of Russia,"* even though what they really meant was an end of militant atheism in Russia. But Our Lady never spoke of the "conversion of Islam." *Rather, taking the name of Fatima, She promised "an era of peace for mankind."*

In Islam, "conversion" is anathema. A Muslim who "converts" to Christianity may be assassinated. If a Muslim should wish to become a Christian in Syria, for example, which is not even an Islamic state (like Iran and Saudi Arabia), it is strictly forbidden. The Muslim would have to leave the country.

The same is true in Turkey. Although it is a lay or secular state, "conversion" to Christianity is strictly forbidden and rigidly enforced. The Armenian massacre by the Turks cries out from the pages of history latent in the Christian-Islamic confrontation which goes back thirteen hundred years.

Now the tide of Islam is rising again. If there is to be a cry to avoid a deadly conflict, it must be in the amazing words of Prince Pahlavi: "*I believe that Mary can bring Islam and Christianity together.*"

Individual Battle Cries

But if we do not have a suitable Battle Cry for the world, we have an abundance of motivating words for *individuals who will respond.*

Those who respond *will have nothing to fear*, no matter what happens. Those who respond will be singularly blessed and will have the presence of Our Lady at the hour of death, "with all the aid and graces needed." Those who respond, Our Lady promised to place like flowers at the throne of God. They will know that they are with the powerful Queen of the World as She moves forward to a great victory.

On the wall of Fatima, two simple words stand out to halt us in our path to corruption and destruction: PRAYER AND PENANCE. These words are translated into three simple practices:

1) Consecration to the Immaculate Heart of Mary;

2) offering up the sacrifices required by daily duty (Our Lady said "This is the penance I now require.");

3) the Rosary.

But while these are the words that say STOP HERE!, another word speaks of *turning back the tide of corruption.*

It translates into a practice we are asked to do only five times in our lives, on five consecutive First Saturdays.

"Remember My Words"

We tend to be fascinated by the words spoken at Fatima concerning future events, especially of possible chastisement. *But there are many other important words Our Lady has spoken upon which we must meditate* in the context of what has already happened and what may happen.

There are now many posters on the wall.

It is the purpose of the monument and museum at the castle of Ourem not only to honor Our Lady

as Queen of the World but to help the world respond to Her command: *"Remember my words."*

We are too often anxious to hear new words and to forget the words already spoken. We tend to overlook the lessons of history engraved, as it were, for all to see in the pictures and statues, which will now be found in this world center of devotion to Our Lady of All Nations.

Her message has not changed since the apparitions to St. Catherine Labouré almost two hundred years ago, and expressed in Her many apparitions and images. It has only become *more urgent and more specific.*

Unveiling of the monument to the Queen of the World at the Fatima castle on the Feast of Our Lady's Queenship in 1996. The ceremony was the focal point of a worldwide commemoration of the golden jubilee of the papal coronation of Our Lady of Fatima as Queen of the World.

CHAPTER ELEVEN

"FATIMA HAS JUST BEGUN"

In her interview with Cardinal Vidal, on October 11, 1993, Sister Lucia said: "*All the wars which have occurred could have been avoided through prayer and sacrifice. This is the reason Our Lady asked for the Communion of Reparation* (on First Saturdays) *and the consecration.*"

She added: "People expect things to happen immediately within their own time frame. But Fatima is still in its third day. *The triumph is an ongoing process.*"

Then, repeating herself, she said: "Fatima is still in its third day. We are now in the post-consecration period. The first day was the apparition period. The second was the post-apparition, pre-consecration period. *The Fatima week has not yet ended.*

"I may not get to see the whole week, as you yourself (speaking to the interpreter, a young man) will not, since you did not live through the first day.

"*Fatima has just begun.* How can one expect it to be over immediately?"

The New Pledge

Cardinal Vidal was the head of a group of Philippine Bishops who sponsored an apostolate of response to the message of Fatima with a pledge, which had been formulated by Sister Lucia in 1946 and which, for almost fifty years, had been promoted throughout the world by the Blue Army.

To this basic pledge (Morning Offering, Scapular and Rosary), the new apostolate added emphasis on the First Saturday Communions of Reparation. Many thousands responded in the Philippines and other countries, especially in the third world. Promotion of the pledge was made by the magazine *Voice of the Sacred Hearts* and by seminars, many of which were attended personally by the Cardinal and the supporting bishops.

After having said: "Fatima has just begun," Lucia said: "The Rosary, which is the most important spiritual weapon we have in these times when the devil is so active, should be recited."

The Cardinal then asked whether the apostolate (with the pledge and the emphasis on First Saturdays) fulfilled Our Lady's requests.

"I believe so," Sister Lucia replied. "This movement shows itself to be the fulfillment of what the Virgin asked. *To promote the Communion of Reparation is the means to combat atheism...* The Virgin is interested in everything (the entire pledge), but particularly in the Communions of Reparation."

This Movement

"This movement," to which Sister Lucia referred, had its origin in a symposium held at Fatima, based on the expression of Pope John Paul II: "The Alliance of the Two Hearts."

Encouraged by the Holy Father, and with the theological basis of this symposium, there developed an apostolate of the Sacred Hearts with a magazine sponsored by a group of Philippine bishops, headed by Cardinal Vidal. It spread rapidly in the third world.

This apostolate, which Sister Lucia said met the conditions of Our Lady of Fatima, stressed the basic pledge of Fatima (Morning Offering, Scapular and Rosary), with fresh emphasis on the First Friday—First Saturday Communions of Reparation, particularly through night vigils.

This new emphasis, she said, was most important: "The Virgin is interested in everything, but particularly in the Communions of Reparation."

New Emphasis for the Third Day

What had been emphasized before this "third day" of Fatima was the Morning Offering (the sanctification of daily duties) as the *most important* part of the Fatima response. Sister Lucia had said, in an interview with the author in July of 1946, that other devotions (like the Rosary and Scapular, which she later described as "inseparable") were *the aids to extend the morning offering throughout the day.* She gave assurance that when enough persons were doing this, Russia would be converted.

At that time, as we mentioned before, she did not stress the devotion of the First Saturdays. She related them to the basic request for sanctification of daily duties (i.e., living the morning offering). When asked if the First Saturdays were important, she replied:

"Yes, because they will cause us once a month to renew our purpose."

So why is such greater emphasis placed on the First Saturday Communions of Reparation *now?* The answer is found in an often overlooked command given by Our Lord, specifically for the time following the change in Russia.

Request of Our Lord

For the change in Russia, it was required that the Pope, together with all the bishops of the world, consecrate that nation to the Immaculate Heart of Mary. And when one Pope after another had failed to make this collegial consecration of Russia, Lucia asked Our Lord, on the command of her confessor, why He insisted that the consecration had to be made in union with all the bishops of the world. Our Lord answered:

"*Because I want the entire Church* to know that this favor (the change in Russia) was obtained *through the Immaculate Heart of My Mother* so that *afterwards, it may extend this devotion of the Five First Saturdays and place devotion to Her Immaculate Heart alongside devotion to My Own Sacred Heart.*"

In a letter to her confessor on May 29, 1930, Sister Lucia repeated that Our Lord promised the change in Russia when the collegial consecration was made. Next, Our Lord said:

"*The Holy Father must then promise that upon the ending of this persecution* (of religion in Russia), *he will approve and recommend the practice of the reparatory devotion* (i.e. the Five First Saturdays)."

So now, the time following the change in Russia, is the time when the Holy Father is to approve and recommend the First Saturday devotion. It is the "day" when whatever happens next in this unfolding Divine saga will depend on how many respond to the basic requests of Fatima and complete the Communions of Reparation.

Four More Days?

This entire interview with Cardinal Vidal in October of 1993 was recorded on both audio and video tape, and therefore is completely accurate. Published in a booklet titled *Two Hours with Sister Lucia,* it must be considered a major development in the Fatima story. In it, Sister Lucia explained that the collegial consecration made on March 25, 1984 was accepted by God. She said that the "conversion" of Russia, which meant the granting of freedom of religion in that country, *was brought about by God.* It brought us into the "third day." What will the fourth day bring?

Must Be With the Pope

In a previous interview with Cardinal Vidal, Sister Lucia had said: "He who is not with the Pope is not with God, and he who wishes to be with God must be with the Pope."

The Cardinal asked why she had said that.

Because of the Cardinal's schedule, this interview took place at night, and it was now almost midnight (11:30 pm), far beyond the normal time for this 83 year old Carmelite to be so occupied.

She seemed surprised by the question, but she reaffirmed that we must be with the Pope because He is Our Lord's representative in our midst.

The Cardinal then offered to conclude the interview with a prayer for the Pope. But, before the prayer could be said, the Cardinal's companion added:"So many people today do not believe…"

"This has always been," Sister Lucia responded, "but *now it is more pronounced.* It is the result of materialism. By this, God is much offended…"

Cardinal Vidal suddenly thought of a final, unexpected question: "Do you have any messages about current apparitions in the world?"

Sister Lucia answered: "We are in union of prayers... God has manifested Himself in miracles... God could also work other miracles... We are ignorant of these mysteries. Therefore, we try to have the capacity to know them."

The Fourth Day

Are we surprised that Sister Lucia said: "Fatima has just begun?"

The first day, the period of the apparitions, lasted only two years. The second day, before the consecration, lasted sixty seven years. What event will signal the end of this third day, the time following the consecration?

Pope John Paul II, in *Crossing the Threshold of Hope,* said: "As we approach the millennium, it seems that *the words of Our Lady of Fatima are nearing their fulfillment.*"

Further, in his subsequent apostolic letter to prepare for the millennium, His Holiness said he did so "*in the hope of the definitive coming of the kingdom.*"

There is a growing expectation today of what Sister Lucia suggested by saying, in answer to the question about other apparitions in the world: "*God could also work other miracles.*"

Rather than speculate what they may be, the burning question of the moment must be: *Is the request of Our Lord for this "third day" being fulfilled?*

Our Lord Himself said that after the consecration, and after the change in Russia (which He would then bring about), *devotion to the Immaculate Heart of His Mother was to be placed alongside devotion to His Own Sacred Heart, especially by means of the First Saturday Communions of Reparation.* Unfortunately, most do not seem to realize the gravity of this need. It therefore seems that the International Center of the Queen of the World at the Fatima Castle is providential. It may occasion a united effort of response.

As we cannot say too often, in his special letter to Fatima on Oct. 13, 1997, the Pope said that Fatima was one of the greatest signs of our time not so much because of the miracle but because it *shows us the alternative* and tells us the *specific response* needed to meet that alternative. Will we choose peace or self-destruction?

Cardinal Vidal thought to ask about recent apparitions of Our Lady and, as we ponder her prudent reply, we think of Fatima as the wall upon which Our Lady, in subsequent apparitions, has placed posters to call our attention to the urgency of Her message.

In that October 13th, 1997 letter, the Pope explained the reason for it all. He said Our Lady of Fatima came with Her specific requests *"to save mankind from itself."*

Not a New Devotion

In Her apparition at Fatima on July 13, 1917, after several prophecies, which ended with the words *"several nations will be annihilated,"* Our Lady said: "To prevent this, I shall come to ask for the consecration of Russia to my Immaculate Heart and for the Communion of Reparation on the First Saturdays."

At that time, this devotion was already known. St. Pius X had granted indulgences for the practice of devotion to the Immaculate Conception on twelve First Saturdays. Seven years later, on June 13 of 1912 (just five years before the second apparition of Fatima), the same Pope granted additional indulgences to encourage this devotion.

On Nov 13, 1920, five years before Our Lady "came back" to ask for this, Pope Benedict XV granted still further indulgences to the First Saturday devotion, at the same time reducing the number of twelve, set by St. Pius X, to eight.

The First Saturday Promise

When Our Lady of Fatima finally "came back" on Dec. 10, 1925, requesting these First Saturday Communions of Reparation, She Herself lowered the number to five. At the same time, She promised to all those who complete the Five First Saturdays: "I will assist, at the hour of death, with the graces necessary..."

This promise implies the *presence* of Our Lady at the hour of death. When we promise to assist at a ceremony or to *assist* at a friend's wedding, do we not mean especially that we will be *present?*

This new promise of Our Lady seems to add another dimension to the promise of salvation attached to the Communions of Reparation in honor of the Sacred Heart on nine consecutive First Fridays. Many more years of experience may be necessary for a definitive judgment, but based on limited observation, the First Saturday promise seems to be the promise of a "happy death."

Example from Estelle Faguette

When Estelle Faguette was dying at Pellevoisin, France, on Nov. 14, 1876, the devil appeared at the foot of her bed. She was so terrified that she drew herself back to the top of the bed despite her extreme weakness.

At the same moment, Our Lady appeared on the other side of the bed. Instantly, Satan withdrew. (See *Her Glorious Title,* pg 95.)

We know that the hour of death can be terrible. It is an hour many fear. What a consolation to have the *promise* that Our Lady will be there!

St. Catherine of Siena heard of a young man condemned to death for political reasons, and who refused to see a priest. She visited him in prison and his despair left him when Catherine was there. But he felt so desolate when she was gone that he made her promise that, "for the sake of God's love, you will be with me when the day of execution comes."

St. Catherine tells us in her diary: "I went with him to Mass and Holy Communion, which he had always avoided. He was afraid of only one thing: that his courage would fail him in the crucial moment. He said: 'Stay with me, do not go from me, and I will be good. I will die happy.'"

When Catherine finally promised to await him at the place of execution, she tells us: "Then his heart was freed from fear, the melancholy in his face changed to gladness, and he said: 'Where does it come from, such great mercy?'"

Catherine was there when he was beheaded. She caught his severed head in her own hands. At once she saw his soul, entering Heaven, turn to look at her, "as a bride does when she comes to the house of her bridegroom."

If it could be such a consolation to have a saint at one's side at the moment of death, what must it be to have at one's side the Queen of Saints, the Mother of God Herself!

The Conditions

When Our Lady of Fatima came to ask for the First Saturday devotion, Lucia (then the only surviving visionary of Fatima) was a postulant in the convent of the Dorothean Sisters in Pontevedra, Spain. It happened on Dec. 10, 1925.

Our Lady entered Lucia's tiny cell with the Child Jesus. Her Heart appeared pierced by many thorns. The Holy Child was elevated so that Lucia could look into His eyes at the same time that she looked into the eyes of His Mother.

He was the first to speak: "Have compassion on the Heart of your most holy Mother, covered with thorns with which ungrateful men pierce it at every moment, and there is no one to make an act of reparation to remove them!"

The space in the little room was so narrow that Our Lady *was resting Her hand on Lucia's shoulder,* making this one of the most intimate of all recorded, approved apparitions. Lucia was struck with the words of the Holy Child, as He referred to Our Lady's suffering heart as *the heart of YOUR Mother!* (Oh, how intimately the thorns and love of Her Heart bind us to His!)

"*Look, my daughter,*" Our Lady now said, "*at my heart surrounded with thorns with which ungrateful men pierce it at every moment by their blasphemies and ingratitude... You at least try to console me.*"

Our Lady then made the great promise to all who would fulfill the following conditions: "On the first Saturday of five consecutive months—confess, receive Holy Communion, recite five decades of the Rosary, and keep me company for fifteen minutes while meditating on the mysteries of the Rosary, with the intention of making reparation to me."

Jesus Comes Back

Six weeks passed. Lucia had told the Prioress about the request of Our Lady and the Holy Child for this First Saturday devotion. The superior replied that there was nothing she could do about it. And without the support of the superior, what could Lucia do? She was filled with concern.

On February 26, 1926, while she was transferring waste from a cesspool to a street sewer, a little boy, who seemed to be passing by, paused at the gate. He seemed sad and lonely. "Don't you have anyone to play with?" she asked.

The boy did not reply. Something about him, and his sadness, caused Lucia to ask if he knew the Hail Mary.

He remained silent, sad. She had her duties to fulfill. Was there any way she could console him?

"Why don't you go around the corner to the Church of St. Mary Major and ask Our Lady to give you the Child Jesus to keep you company?"

At that the little boy was transformed. It was Jesus, just as she had seen Him six weeks before, with Our Lady, in her little room.

What Is Being Done?

Although transformed, He was still sad, as He asked:

"What is being done to promote the devotion to the Immaculate Heart of My Mother in the world?"

Pausing in astonishment from her lowly work, and struck by the same sadness, Lucia answered: "I told the Mother Superior and she said there was nothing she could do."

"*Of herself, no,*" Jesus replied, "*but with My Grace, she can do it all.*"

To set an example to the world, Pope John Paul II has personally led the First Saturday Rosary, month after month, year in and year out, during the last years of his Pontificate.

But it seems that this devotion depends on each of us.

When the Holy Child said that even the Dorothean Prioress could, with His Grace, do all that was needed to promote this devotion, was He not speaking to each of us? With His Grace, can we not all become successful apostles in proclaiming Our Lady's great promise and the desire of the Sacred Hearts for this simple devotion?

Much depends upon it.

When Our Lady first announced this devotion, She had made a series of prophecies ending in the words: "*Several entire nations will be annihilated.*" Then She said that She would come to ask for this devotion, these First Saturday Communions of Reparation, "*TO PREVENT THIS.*"

From the time Our Lady said this at Fatima, on July 13, 1917, little Jacinta often said: "I am so grieved not to be able to receive Communion in reparation for the sins committed against the Immaculate Heart of Mary!"

But why is Holy Communion the object of reparation? Why on First Saturdays, and why accompanied by the Rosary, fifteen minutes of meditation, and confession, even if we are not in mortal sin?

What Most Offends Their Sacred Hearts

Anything which offends the Heart of Jesus offends the Heart of His Mother. The greatest offenses are those directly against Our Lord, in the Sacrament of His Love.

Our Lady said at Pellevoisin: "What most offends my Immaculate Heart are *careless Communions.*"

Today, how many Communions are not only careless but even sacrilegious! Our Lord had asked for Communions of Reparation to His Sacred Heart on nine First Fridays. And now He reminds us of the same thorns piercing the Heart of His Mother. He asks for Communions of Reparation to HER Immaculate Heart. We are asked to prepare ourselves for that Communion by confession, fifteen minutes of meditation, and by praying the Rosary.

What Most Consoles Their Sacred Hearts

More and more generous souls are saying: "Dear Lord, You ask so little on the First Fridays to console Your Heart, You ask so little on First Saturdays to console *our* Mother's Heart.

"We will give Your Sacred Hearts not just those few hours but the entire night! We will begin on First Friday evening, in honor of Your Sacred Heart, and keep You company in the Sacrament of Your Love to the morning of First Saturday, in honor of the Immaculate Heart of Mary!"

These are known as the Vigils of the Two Hearts. Thousands of generous souls throughout the world are now making this response. Some feel it is this which will tip the balance of God's Justice.

Our Lord said to Lucia in March, 1939: "Ask, ask again insistently, for the promulgation of the Communion of

Reparation in honor of the Immaculate Heart of Mary on the First Saturdays. The time is coming when the rigor of My Justice will punish the crimes of diverse nations. Some of them will be annihilated. At last, the severity of My Justice will fall severely on those who want to destroy My Reign in souls." (*Documentos*, pg. 465.)

Why Five?

We noted before that St. Pius X indulgenced the devotion for twelve First Saturdays. Granting still further indulgences, Pope Benedict XV made it eight. Our Lady, extending the conditions, made it five. Why?

Sister Lucia explains: "While in the chapel with Our Lord part of the night between the 29th and 30th of May, 1930, while speaking to Our Good Lord about this question, I felt myself being more possessed by the Divine Presence and the following was made known to me:

"Jesus said: 'My daughter, the reason is simple. There are five ways by which people offend and blaspheme against the Immaculate Heart of Mary:

1) Blasphemies against Her Immaculate Conception;

2) Blasphemies against Her virginity;

3) Blasphemies against Her Divine Maternity, refusing at the same time to accept Her as the Mother of all mankind;

4) Those who try publicly to implant in the hearts of children indifference, contempt, and even hatred against this Immaculate Mother;

5) Those who insult Her directly in Her sacred images.

"'Here, My daughter, are the reasons why the Immaculate Heart of Mary compelled Me to ask for this little act of reparation and, due to it, to move My Mercy to forgive those souls who had the misfortune of offending Her. As for you, try unceasingly with all your prayers and sacrifices to move Me to Mercy toward those poor souls.'"

Must It Be On Saturday?

The reason Saturday is "Our Lady's Day" is because it was on the Saturday after Good Friday that Our Lady's passion continued. She suffered not only the aftermath of Calvary but the knowledge that Her Jesus was dead. She longed to be with Him in the tomb. At the same time, She suffered because the apostles were scattered. She worried especially about Judas and Peter. She was now the Mother of the Church.

Therefore, it is ideal to fulfill all four conditions of the First Saturday on the day itself, all with the intention of making reparation—of helping to remove the thorns encircling Her maternal Heart.

However, Our Lord told Lucia that, for a good reason, His priests may change the day if, for example, no priest is available on the Saturday, but only on the next day—a Sunday. It has also become common practice for the all night vigils to choose the Saturday after First Friday on the rare occasions when a Saturday may fall on the first day of the month.

It is generally understood that the confession may be within seven days, provided the recipient of First Saturday Communion is in the state of Grace. But again, it is advisable to go to confession on the First Saturday (or prior to the First Friday Communion), if possible.

A great advantage of the night vigil is that one fulfills the requests of the Sacred Heart for First Friday, and of the Immaculate Heart for First Saturday, at the same time. And during the night, there is ample time for confession, for the fifteen minute meditation, for the Rosary, and above all for the making of a truly worthy Communion of Reparation. Fittingly, the vigils have come to be known as "The Night of Love." (For further information on the vigils, see book of this same name, *The Night Of Love*, available from the 101 Foundation.)

"Keep Me Company"

One of the wonders of the First Saturdays is the invitation of Our Lady to "*keep me company* for fifteen minutes, while meditating on the mysteries of the Rosary."

At the moment of the epiphany of Jesus in the temple, there was an epiphany of Our Lady's Heart. While recognizing the Savior of the world, the prophet Simeon saw Our Lady's Heart. "*Your own Heart a sword will pierce,*" the holy man exclaimed, *"that out of many hearts thoughts might be revealed."*

This prophecy is fulfilled on the First Saturday as we keep Mary company, as we share in the mysteries of Her Heart and the Heart of Jesus. It is not so much that we keep Our Lady company as that She keeps company with us!

The great Marian apostle of Poland, Anatol Kaszczuk, exclaimed: "Oh, how I look forward to the First Saturdays when Our Lady shares with us the mysteries of Her Heart!"

It is a blessed experience.

"These Souls Will Be Beloved"

In the apparition of June 13, 1917, Our Lady told the children of Fatima: "Jesus wishes to use you to make Me known and loved. *He wishes to establish in the world devotion to My Immaculate Heart.* To those who embrace it, I promise salvation, and these souls will be beloved by God like flowers placed by Me to adorn His Throne."

In February, 1999, it was announced by the postulator of the two younger children of Fatima, Francis and Jacinta, that Rome had approved the cause for their beatification. The message of reparation to the Immaculate Heart of Mary, which made them saints, was at the heart of the entire Fatima message.

When Our Lady promised in 1917 to come "soon" to take Francis and Jacinta to Heaven, Lucia asked sadly: "Must I stay here alone?"

Our Lady answered: "No, My daughter. *I will never forsake you. My Immaculate Heart will be your consolation and the way that will lead you to God."*

Do we wish to be souls beloved of God? Do we wish to be like flowers placed by Our Lady Herself to adorn His Throne? Do we wish never to be alone, always having Her Immaculate Heart as our consolation and the way that will lead us to God?

These are the blessings of this devotion!

What is more, when enough persons are fulfilling the basic requests of Our Lady by means of the Scapular, Rosary, and Morning Offering, and by completing the Five First Saturdays, we will see more wonders in the world like the sudden downfall of the Soviet Union. *Annihilation of nations may be prevented.* The reign of the Sacred Hearts, promised at Fatima and confirmed by Our Lady of All Nations, will prevail among the nations of the world.

Principal sources:
Her Own Words to the Nuclear Age,
> by John Haffert (101 Foundation, 1990)
Documentos de Fatima, by Father Martins, S.J.
Catherine of Siena, by Sigrid Undset (S&W, 1954), pg. 199
Osservatore Romano, Oct. 1, 1997
Two Hours with Sister Lucia, by Carlos Evaristo (Fatima, 1993)

The apparition of Our Lady and the Holy Child, Dec. 10, 1927, in which They asked for the devotion of the five First Saturdays.

CHAPTER TWELVE

THE NEW BATTLE CRY

Although given new emphasis now in the 21st century, devotion to the Hearts of Jesus and Mary is very old in the Church. Some saints spoke of the Hearts of Jesus and Mary as though they were one single heart, one single flame of love. Jesus had prayed that we all might be one, as He and the Father are one. This prayer was fulfilled in Mary. It is the Will of God that it be fulfilled in us.

Will that be the triumph of the Immaculate Heart of Mary in the world?

To the surprise of many, in his encyclical *Tertio Millennio Adveniente*, Pope John Paul II spoke of entering the new millennium "*in the hope of the definitive coming of the Kingdom.*" He had said in his book *Crossing the Threshold of Hope* that he expected victory, and that it would come through Mary.

This "smell of victory" is in the air.

In one of the most recent apparitions of Our Lady sanctioned by the Church, Our Lady presented Herself as the Queen of the World, the "Lady of All Nations," who had come now to achieve a final victory. Although the apparitions did not receive ecclesiastical sanction until May 31, 1996, the prayer, which She requested, had been approved and distributed to every corner of the world during the previous forty years. A picture on the front of the Japanese version of this prayer was used as the model for the statue of Our Lady of Akita.

Following those millions of prayers, disseminated in dozens of different languages, there has been a worldwide response to the request made in Amsterdam for definition by the Church that Our Lady is Co-Redemptrix, Mediatrix, and Advocate.

Almost unbelievable opposition developed to the definition of these beliefs which Catholics had held for centuries. *We had struck a flash point in the struggle between the Woman in the Sun and the great Dragon.*

The Last Great Sign?

Our Lady of All Nations had made a remarkable promise. She said that when the dogma is proclaimed, Her victory will take place.

In other words, just as the collegial consecration of Russia was the sign that Russia would be converted, so the proclamation of this dogma will be the sign of the triumph of the Immaculate Heart. There will be an era of peace for mankind.

Mother Angelica, of EWTN, expressed the belief that it will be an era of the Eucharist. St. Catherine Labouré, to whom Our Lady appeared as Queen at the beginning of the Marian age, prophesied:

"Oh, how wonderful it will be to hear Our Lady hailed as Queen of the World! It will be a time of triumph, joy, and well being."

What Was the Battle Cry?

What motivated some five million Catholics, including some 500 Cardinals and Bishops, to sign a petition for the dogma?

Perhaps in the prayer of Our Lady of All Nations, we may discover the Battle Cry for today. It reads:

"O, Lord Jesus Christ, Son of the Father, send now Your Spirit over the earth. Let the Holy Spirit live in the hearts of all peoples, so that they may be kept free from corruption, catastrophe and war. May the Lady of All Nations, who once was Mary, be our advocate. Amen."

Instead of "catastrophe and war," some translations read simply: "destruction." This is the word the Pope used in his act of consecration of the world to the Immaculate Heart of Mary. It is the word he used in his Oct. 13, 1997 Fatima letter. It is a word which, perhaps better than "catastrophe and war," echoes the prophecy: "Several entire nations will be annihilated."

That is what Our Lady has come to prevent! That is what can be obtained if enough will still respond to Her requests!

She said at Akita:

"So far I have been able to hold back the chastisement." She did this by offering the passion of Her Son to the Father, and by the prayers and sacrifices of a few who respond generously.

What call must now go out to the world, to Christian and Muslim, to believer and unbeliever? What will be the new Battle Cry? Could it be: "*Save the world from corruption and destruction!*" Is it not too late!?

Other Posters

We have confined ourselves in this little book to the message of Fatima and the two posters of Amsterdam and Akita, which have been declared credible by Church Authority.

But meanwhile, some twenty million pilgrims have gone to Medjugorje. They are now scattered through the world with the call of Her message of peace. Other "great signs" have been predicted at Medjugorje, and also at Garabandal.

While the Church cannot speak of the authenticity of these events until the predicted signs take place, *they accentuate the message of Fatima.* They do not add anything substantial. But they have had considerable impact on local populations and in the world.

Chastisement Preview?

Our Lady spoke at Fatima of the annihilation of "several entire nations." At Akita, She said:

"Fire from the sky will wipe out *a great part of humanity.*"

In Rwanda, one tenth of the population was horribly slaughtered, and the aftermath seemed an even greater tragedy with 175,000 people locked in communal prisons, as many as seventy in a room fifteen by fifteen feet. *In the first eleven months of 1998, 2,272 of the jailed, accused of massacre, died of AIDS.*

Our Lady at Fatima had said: "The cause of war is sin." And when the means She offers to draw men up from the quagmire of sin are rejected, are we surprised to see the intervention of God's Justice? It has been said that if God did not punish some of our nations today, He would have to apologize to Sodom and Gomorrha.

In Bosnia, the small country of Medjugorje, Fr. Franjo Radman said: "to be a priest in Bosnia now is a terrible thing. One horror story follows another until it seems *as if there is nothing left in the world except horror.*"

As in Rwanda, the horrors in Bosnia began exactly ten years after the reported apparitions of Our Lady.

Too Terrible to Seem Real

As Muslim and Christian Arabs in Israel, in the last decade of the twentieth century, seemed to unite in a struggle for a Palestinian State, so at first Catholics and Muslims were united in the face of Serbian aggression in the beginning of the conflict in former Yugoslavia.

But horror seemed contagious. Muslims began to fight Christians as well as Serbs, and with the same degree of atrocity. Murder became rampant. Sides became blurred. It was as though *hell had suddenly become present* on earth.

She spoke of peace. Marija, one of the visionaries, said it was only after the war began that they understood. She was saying, as in Her apparition in Cuapa, Nicaragua (approved by the local Bishop): "Make peace where you are or you will not have peace." She insisted on the praying of the Rosary to obtain peace where we are, and *then* in the world. She had said over and over that prayer and fasting can "stop wars," and it was only when their little nation did not respond as She asked that they experienced a horror *they could have stopped.*

Bitter Lesson

It is sad to admit that at Medjugorje, there was no peace between the Bishop and the local Franciscans. There was a dispute over jurisdiction of some parishes. The local bishop's conflict with the Franciscans who had the Medjugorje parish may have influenced his rejection of the apparitions, creating great confusion among the faithful.

Now, ten years after Our Lady first came there, the Bishop's nearby city of Mostar was largely in ruins. Another bishop was in charge. And the Franciscans were mostly in exile.

Before the war, there had been eighteen friaries in Bosnia. On the day of Heather Parson's interview with him in 1993, he could name only three that he could reach. Four had been destroyed. Twenty parish churches and houses had also been destroyed, along with forty small chapels. The fate of all the others was in doubt.

A couple of weeks earlier, he had managed to get through to one of the former parishes, about sixty miles away. He found the Catholic community *almost extinct*. The church and monastery were damaged beyond use. The Muslims were in complete control.

It could all have been prevented. Fault was probably on both sides, but peace was not made. And should not the clergy have set the example?

Our Heavenly Mother is calling for response not just from the laity of the world. Does She not expect it even more from those entrusted with the care of souls? Sometimes, sad to say, they seem to be the ones least inclined to listen.

Anxious Mother of All

At Medjugorje, Our Lady did not give dire warnings (as in Rwanda). She merely spoke of peace, of the need of making peace in our own families and parishes, and of conversion. Only when there was not sufficient response and the horrors began was Her message understood.

She had come to speak of peace in order to show how it could be obtained. And while She stressed praying of the Rosary, She also *asked for special souls* who would pray and fast, *beginning with three hours a day,* in order to arrive at making every moment of the day a prayer. She wanted the members of the parish She was visiting, day after day, to become saints. *She wanted total commitment from them to make up for the lack of commitment in the places where Her voice was not heard.*

In one of Her apparitions, She designated a Muslim in Medjugorje as a saintly person, very dear to God. *She was as lovingly concerned for Her Muslim children as for all others.*

All the posters placed on the wall of Fatima since 1917 proclaim the same message. It is the cry of an anxious, loving Mother who sees millions of Her children caught in the quagmire of sin. She sees millions swallowed by a tidal wave of pornography and promiscuity, with fornication begetting further sins of broken families and killing of infants in the womb.

This, She said at Fatima, *is the cause of war.* And so, She comes to save us ALL by drawing us to Heart of Jesus, through Her own Immaculate Heart.

Out of the Quagmire

The first step to be taken, up and out of the quagmire, is *an act of consecration to Her Immaculate Heart.*

At Fatima, She said:

"God wishes to establish in the world devotion to My Immaculate Heart... Finally my Immaculate Heart will triumph, Russia will be converted and an era of peace will be granted to mankind."

The Pope said in his Fatima letter of Oct. 13, 1997 so often quoted in these pages:

"From Fatima, She extends Her mantle over the whole world."

At Garabandal, She is reported to have said: "I have come for all my children with the intention of drawing all into our Hearts... **I hold them all beneath my mantle.**"

At Medjugorje, calling for conversion, She said: "I am with you and **I place all under my mantle.**"

This is the first desire of the anxious, merciful Mother: to have us all beneath Her mantle. She wants us close to Her Immaculate Heart. She wants to shield us from the satanic tidal wave of evil.

But, just signing a pledge and sending one's name to be placed in Her Heart at Fatima will not be enough. "Consecration" means "to be set aside." It means to recognize that She extends Her mantle to us and we, in turn, *take refuge beneath it.* We can profess this by wearing Her Scapular *as a constant reminder* that we are "set aside." We have renounced the quagmire and taken refuge beneath the mantle of the Immaculate.

Perhaps only this, if enough persons responded, could turn the tide. But the quagmire clings. *She extends two special aids to draw us up: The Rosary and the offering of the sacrifices demanded by our every day duties.* Those are the basic requests of Fatima. They have not proved enough. Now a fourth "lift" from the quagmire is given: the devotion of the Five First Saturdays.

The Special Souls

One of the greatest signs of hope in all that Our Lady has said is that, "so far," She has been able to hold back the annihilation of nations in two ways:

1) "by offering to the Father the sufferings of the Son on the Cross, His Precious Blood;"

2) "by beloved souls who console Him and form a cohort of victim souls."

She is also calling for those who will "go all the way." There is a need for daily communicants, for the chaplet of Mercy, for adoration of the Blessed Sacrament, for fasting, for three hours of prayer a day and beyond!

A New Cry

A new cry needs to go forth to all the those consecrated to the Immaculate Heart of Mary: to become "beloved souls" forming a cohort, a special task force of Her spiritual army, offering *everything* in union with Her Sorrowful and Immaculate Heart.

This *totus tuus* way has been led by Pope John Paul II, by word and example. Afflicted by much suffering (an assassination attempt, a broken hip, etc.), he said: "I saw that the Pope had to lead the way also by suffering."

Perhaps when the messages of Medjugorje are evaluated and formally sanctioned by the Church, they will be found to say just this: that the degree of sanctity needed to enable the Immaculate to turn back the tidal wave of sexual and social evil is a "conversion" through *daily Mass, prayer groups, spiritual guidance, retreats.* (Marthe Robin brought the message of five day lay retreats.)

Our Lady Herself has already begun to draw many of those consecrated to Her Heart to "go all the way." An example is the Mary Queen of Peace "Communion," aimed at *daily* conversion through living the *totus tuus* consecration. Handbooks of daily prayer and meditation have been published in several languages. This is only one of several similar organized efforts for total living of the message of prayer, fasting, spiritual reading (especially Scripture), confession, and the Eucharist. (*Communion*, 150 rang St. Jean Baptiste, Sainte Aurélie, Québec, Canada GOM 1MO.)

We need a cohort of souls willing to *go the whole way.* **To enter the triumphant era of the Divine Will, we must have not only those who make the consecration, but who make it totally.**

So what will be the new Battle Cry? And what call shall we send out from the Fatima Castle, from the International Center of the Queen of the World?

Begin With the Name

Although we might like to ask for ALL that Our Lady asks, we can begin by giving free copies of the picture and prayer of Our Lady of all Nations, touched to the miraculous statue (shown on page 47) which for fifty years has gone through the world as the "Messenger of Her Royalty" (Pope Pius XII). We hope that those who receive it may also respond to the three *basic* requests of Our Lady.

We will have their names placed on a computer disc in the statue of the Immaculate Heart at the Fatima Castle, International Center of the Queen of the World, to be remembered in the prayers of all the other participants throughout the world. *And, we can invite them to communicate with centers in their own countries.* If they wish, they can in this way, keep posted on events and encouraged to persevere. (In U.S.: PO Box 29870, Wichita, KS, 67208.)

What will be the battle cry? Let it be the words of the prayer taught to us by Our Lady of All Nations:

"TO SAVE FROM CORRUPTION AND DESTRUCTION!"

We cry out to Islam:

"Pray with us to the Immaculate! Join us in Her Immaculate Heart to save us *all* from corruption and destruction!"

Christians, we are living in the times of Genesis 3:15, and of Apocalypse 12! As the Woman clothed with the sun took refuge from the dragon in the desert, let us take refuge in Her Immaculate Heart!

It is still not too late.

City of Mostar, episcopal See of Medjugorje.

The remains of Saints Peter and Paul church in Mostar.

Chapter Thirteen

THE ELITE CORPS

We have two hopes of preventing horrors like those of Rwanda and Bosnia from engulfing the world. One is that the number of those responding to the basic requests of Fatima will reach a sufficient number. The other is that the cohort of generous souls, who "go all the way," will become sufficiently strong.

The basis of our hope is response to the basic message and the First Saturday Communions of Reparation. But while those two are our priority, we are very much aware of the other call, the higher call, to which only those who respond to the basics may be expected to respond. Our Lady did not say that She had been able so far to hold back from the world a catastrophe "worse than the deluge" because so many had made the basic pledge but because of the "cohort" of special souls who had become *totus tuus*.

Shortly before writing this book, I wrote three others aimed at developing the cohort: *Now the Woman Shall Conquer, Her Glorious Title,* and *You, Too, Go Into My Vineyard.* The second of those books, *Her Glorious Title,* demonstrates how the basic pledge of Fatima puts a soul on the ascent of Carmel, the ascent to great sanctity. Many other books also explain how to become a *totus tuus* person for the victory of the Queen of the World.

The First Saturday devotion is the way to begin. Most effective are the First Friday—First Saturday vigils.

A Night To Save The World

We began by asking whether it was too late for us to respond, as it has proved too late for Bosnia and Rwanda.

We were asking, in effect, whether nuclear destruction of a large part of the world (which seems to be what Our Lady of all Nations predicts as the alternative) can be prevented.

Dr. Joseph Rotblat, Nobel Prize atomic scientist, said: "*The only way for the world to avoid nuclear destruction is to END war.*" In his opinion, and in the opinion of many, it cannot be avoided unless we can stop war, because ultimately the most destructive weapons are sure to be used.

But, "*wars are caused by sin,*" said Our Lady at Fatima. And how do we get rid of sin? Do we have any *other* hope than that given by Our Lady of putting an end to the tidal wave of sin in the world? *Is there any other hope of saving the world by God's merciful Grace rather than by fire?*

"Time is Coming"

Jesus said, as a part of the Fatima message:

"The time is coming when the rigor of My Justice will punish the crimes of various nations. Some of them will be annihilated." (*Documentos*, pg. 465.)

Appearing with Our Lady, as She asked for the First Saturday Communions of Reparation, Jesus said:

"Have pity on the Heart of your most holy Mother, covered with thorns with which ungrateful men pierce it at every moment, **and there is no one to make an act of reparation** to remove them."

He also said: "*I desire that devotion to the Immaculate Heart of My Mother be placed alongside devotion to My Own Sacred Heart.*"

Almost Perfect Response

An all night vigil, from the First Friday evening (day of the Sacred Heart) to the First Saturday morning (day of the Immaculate Heart), would seem the almost perfect response to the Hearts of Jesus and Mary for reparation. It seems to fulfill in a special way the wish of Our Lord "that devotion to the Immaculate Heart of My Mother be placed alongside devotion to My Own Sacred Heart."

Praising these vigils, Pope John XXIII said: "This is the cloister brought into the world!"

Cardinal O'Connor of New York, speaking on the occasion of the 25th anniversary of First Friday to First Saturday vigils in a parish next to Madison Square Garden, said:

"The Church owes all of you (vigilers) a great debt...not only the Church in New York but *in the entire world.*" (*VOICE*, July-Aug. 1994, pg. 16.)

"Our Lord Knows!"

Thousands are now making these vigils all around the world. Yet amazingly, few Catholics even know they are happening. If they did, would not many more participate?

Cardinal O'Connor, in the message mentioned above, said to the vigilers: "Very few of those whom the world considers important *would have any idea* that you are here now (making this vigil before the Blessed Sacrament) and will be here through the night. But *Our Lord knows.*"

Yes, He knows.

And His Sacred Heart is consoled not only by the adoration and the First Friday Communion His Heart asked of us, but also by our response to His plea to have pity on the Heart of His Mother and ours with the First Saturday Communion.

Fr. Armand Dasseville, O.F.M. Cap., explained:

"Night vigilers pray in reparation for the wrongs in society and to obtain special graces and mercy for a generally sinful and sick world... *The vigils identify with Jesus and Mary in the redemption of the world.*"

Beginning of the Cohort

These vigils, beginning on First Friday, offer to the Father the sufferings of His Son on the Cross, His Precious Blood, and they give Him "**beloved souls who console Him.**" They are at least the beginning of "a cohort of victim souls." (*Meaning of Akita*, pg. 7.)

Such is the importance of these vigils, these nights of reparation to Their Hearts on the very days They have requested: the First Friday and the First Saturday. They asked for only about an hour on each of those days. But a few generous souls cry out: "Oh, Beloved Hearts of my Savior and my Mother! Not just an hour, but the entire night!"

In addition to the First Friday and First Saturday Communions of Reparation, the vigils provide for *Eucharistic Adoration,* which is especially powerful against the evils of our time. At Fatima, the angel taught the children to pray:

> *"O Most Holy Trinity, Father, Son, and Holy Spirit! I adore Thee profoundly. I offer Thee the Body, Blood, Soul and Divinity of Our Lord Jesus Christ, present in all the Tabernacles of the world in reparation for the outrages, sacrileges, and indifference by which He is offended. By the infinite merits of the Sacred Heart of Jesus and the Immaculate Heart of Mary, I beg the conversion of poor sinners."*

Our Lady inspired the children of Fatima to Eucharistic adoration to such a degree that "to console the hidden Jesus" became the central motive in the life of Blessed Francisco. She made all the children aware of the true Presence in the Eucharist.

"Our Lady constantly asked for adoration," Marija told Heather Parsons in the book already cited. "She said that in adoration, we meet God, and when we meet God in a moment of adoration, we grow hugely in the spiritual life."

We begin to take our place in that cohort, helping Our Lady to hold back chastisement from the world and to turn back the tide of evil.

Marija said: "Our Lady said that while we meet God every day in our prayer, we meet Him in a special way in the Eucharist. We meet the living God, Jesus alive and living within us. In this way, we can really become His instruments for the conversion of the world." (pg. 158.)

The Prime Condition

But while the First Saturday devotion and the vigils are so important, we find the Rosary at the heart of these devotions. The Rosary is not an option. She told the children of Fatima: "You *must* pray the Rosary." She insisted on the Rosary in all Her modern apparitions. All the posters on the wall repeat the message: *The Rosary is a prime condition for our personal conversion, and for Her triumph.*

The Rosary opens us to the experience of prayer in the mysteries of the Hearts of Jesus and Mary. It is known to lead even to contemplative prayer.

In a summary of the message of Our Lady at Medjugorje, the author of *Marija* said it was "to open hearts completely to the love of God, to live the life to which He has called them, and in doing so, *to use every aid or weapon at their disposal.*"

At Medjugorje, She also mentioned the Scapular. But Marija said: "The Rosary is especially important. Once when I was asked to put the question to Our Lady what did She recommend to priests, She answered: '*All you priests, pray the Rosary. Dedicate your time to the Rosary.*' This was just after She had called on everyone to pray the Rosary because *with this,* She said, *we would be able to overcome all the adversities that Satan is trying to inflict on the Catholic Church.*"

She added thoughtfully, "I think that some of the priests were surprised. I don't think that this was the answer they were expecting. But our Lady has often reminded us that the Rosary is a powerful prayer."

In her Oct. 11, 1993 interview, Sister Lucia said: "*The Rosary is the most important spiritual weapon we have in these times when the devil is so active.*"

Unfortunately, many do not know how to say it properly.

"One In Their Love"

CHAPTER FOURTEEN

MAKE IT COME ALIVE!

B lessed José Maria Escriva asked: "What is the first thing necessary for devotion to Mary?" The founder of Opus Dei answered his own question:

"It is to realize that She is alive."

Her body is not moldering in some grave awaiting resurrection. It has been assumed gloriously into Heaven. Her real, maternal heart is beating with love for us. She appears in our world. She calls us under Her mantle. She invites us to keep company with Her, meditating on the mysteries of the Rosary on the first Saturday of the month. She waits to share with us, in each Rosary, the mysteries of Her Heart...and to hear our requests.

First Words at Lourdes

It is interesting that, when Our Lady first appeared at Lourdes, She did not speak. There was silence.

Bernadette, wondering what to say or do, noticed that Our Lady had a Rosary on Her wrist. So she took out her own rosary and began to pray it.

As she did so, Our Lady took Her rosary and *counted the beads* with the little saint. Only at the end of the first decade did Our Lady of Lourdes speak Her first words. She joined Bernadette in saying:

"*Glory be to the Father, to the Son, and to the Holy Spirit.*"

Two Simple Ways

There are two simple ways to make the Rosary meaningful, perhaps even "exciting," to the point that one would look forward eagerly to saying it.

The first is *to know that Our Lady is listening.* The second is to know *what you want to ask of Her* when you say: "Pray for us sinners."

It is difficult to say which of the two is more important. They go together.

We are greatly helped in being aware of Our Lady's presence if we have a lovely picture or statue to remind us of Her living presence in Heaven. At the same time, we must be aware that *Heaven is as close as love.* We believe in the "communion" of saints.

Other aids are sacramentals, especially the Scapular, which not only symbolizes the mantle of Mary over us but is a sign of belonging to Her in a special way.

The Thoughts of Her Heart

The moment we take our Rosary into our hands, let us think of Our Lady appearing to St. Bernadette. Let us remember that at the moment the little saint began to say her Rosary, *Our Lady began to count the beads with her.*

Our Lady, who has asked us insistently to pray the Rosary, *is waiting for this prayer from us.* The moment we take our Rosary in hand, we give joy to Her maternal Immaculate Heart. She is at once present to us in a special way.

But it is not in the counting of beads that our hearts touch Her Heart. It is in the mysteries.

When Jesus was presented in the temple, at the same time that God manifested Him as Savior to the prophet Simeon, He also manifested the Heart of His Mother. The prophet exclaimed: "Your own heart a sword will pierce, *that out of many hearts thoughts may be revealed.*"

That prophecy comes alive in the Rosary.

Our Lady asked us to KEEP HER COMPANY once a month for just fifteen minutes to THINK about the mysteries, so that we might begin to say the Rosary meaningfully.

The more we know about each mystery (from reading Scripture or books about the life of Our Lord, such as *Poem of the Man-God*), the more effectively we can place ourselves in the mystery, imagining the actual places and events.

That is the first key to making the Rosary *come alive.*

Have an Intention!

The next key, as we have said, is to have *an intention* for each prayer. It is to ask (in the light of each mystery) *for what is most needed at that moment in our lives.*

An example of how effective this can be is shown in the book *Sex And The Mysteries*, over 300 pages just on this one virtue! (See Appendix I.)

No one can know how powerful this is without actually having something specific for which to say *"Pray for us sinners."* And no one can really understand how great is Our Lady's gift of the Rosary without trying it.

It may not at first be easy to think of an intention for each prayer (each Ave, each Pater, each Gloria) in the light of a particular mystery, but Our Lady is waiting and longing to help us! She invited us on the First Saturdays to keep Her company as we try.

In the beginning, or indeed whenever we find it difficult to think of intentions, we can always pray for the *seven gifts of the Holy Spirit*, and in the last three Aves, ask for *Faith, Hope, and Charity.*

It is easy to memorize the gifts: Wisdom, Understanding, Knowledge, Piety, Perseverance, Fear of the Lord, and Fortitude (if one memorizes the first three, then one can remember two beginning with "P" and two with "F").

Everyone needs the gifts of the Holy Spirit. And we find all seven gifts, plus the theological virtues, in their perfection, in EVERY mystery of the Rosary.

To Avoid Seven Sins, Pray for Us!

Another easy way is to think of *the seven capital sins.* We learned them by heart when we studied for our First Communion: pride, covetousness, lust, anger, gluttony, envy, and sloth. And again, after praying to overcome each one in the light of the mystery, we can pray the *last three Aves for Faith, Hope, and Love.* Just this simple method is enough to say the Rosary meaningfully the rest of our lives.

In a meeting with Sister Lucia in 1946, we began a four hour interview by saying: "Of course we know that the Rosary is the most important request of Our Lady of Fatima."

At once, Sister Lucia corrected this. She said that what is MOST important is the fulfillment of our daily duties. The Rosary is important because *it is an aid both to the fulfillment and sanctification of our acts of each day.*

Our Lady taught the children to pray the Rosary this way. She taught them to see their own lives in the mysteries and to ask for the graces they needed to sanctify their daily duties. They saw all this in the light from Her Heart.

If we wish to pray the Rosary effectively, we must put ourselves in that light, in the PRESENCE of our Mother, and with each prayer, *ask for a specific grace which will help us to sanctify all that we say and do.*

Everyone needs to overcome the seven capital sins. The opposite virtues, together with the three theological virtues, readily lend themselves to petitions in every prayer of all the mysteries.

The Beatitudes

It is also effective to pray for the beatitudes. Perhaps many of us never think of them, even though they are SO important! In the light of the mysteries, they can have an enormous influence on our lives.

Here they are listed, with the promised rewards in parenthesis:

THIRST for Justice (Filled);

MERCIFUL (Mercy);

MEEK (Inherit the Earth);

MOURN (Comforted);

PURE in heart (See God)

POOR in spirit (Heaven);

PEACEMAKERS (Love of God);

PERSECUTED (Heaven).

A sentence which can help us remember the beatitudes, until we know them by heart, is the little phrase:

Thirst for Mercy, Purity and Peace. Two others begin with the first letter "M" (Meek and Mourn), and two with "P" (Poor in spirit and Persecuted).

Understanding These Intentions

Many of the saints have meditated on the beatitudes and tell us what Our Lord meant when He called "HAPPY" those who are meek, poor in spirit, pure in heart, persecuted, merciful, accused falsely, mourn, and weep.

While in the old testament, we lived by ten "DO NOTS," in the new testament, He is inviting us to eight happy "DO'S."

To thirst for Justice is to thirst for God. This is the sum total of the first Commandment. If we DESIRE God, we love Him. And He will fulfill our desire. Gentleness in our dealings with others applies especially to those in authority (including parents), that they do not deal in a domineering way but in a caring, gentle manner.

Meekness in subjects, like gentleness in exercising authority, is rewarded HERE ON THIS EARTH. In a sense it becomes its own reward. "The meek shall inherit the earth." Those who deal with others in haughtiness and pride may be obeyed, but they are resented and often revolted against by those whom they treat abusively. But those who deal in gentleness and meekness are loved. (How well these virtues are exemplified in the mysteries of the Rosary!)

Those who mourn and weep will be comforted not only in Heaven but also here and now, if they accept their sorrow and tears without rebelling. Sorrow and tears mature us and draw us close to the Divine Reality. Hence, those who weep are rewarded with happiness, with the consolation and comfort of God's Love in their lives. Indeed, happy are they!

The merciful, those who forgive, will be forgiven by God.

Those accused falsely and calumniated will be counted among the prophets and saints who suffered similarly, as did Our Lord Himself. If they bear this injustice with humility and acceptance, happy are they!

It is interesting that only two of the beatitudes are rewarded specifically with the promise of Heaven: poverty of spirit and persecution borne with patience.

To be poor in spirit is to prefer the things of Heaven to those of earth. It means to be detached from the wealth we have, whether great or small, using it well. Happy are they!

What a joy to pray for these blessings in our lives! And how wonderfully the mysteries of the Rosary show us the blessedness we can so easily obtain by asking Our Lady. She is the perfect exemplar of all the beatitudes, and She longs to help us obtain them.

Oh! Blessed gift of the Rosary! Happy, indeed, then are we!

What Virtue Do We Need?

As in the case of all Rosary meditations, the more we know about our own spiritual needs, the more effective our Rosary will be. And what we must know above all are:

1) What we need now in our lives to enable us to fulfill and sanctify our daily duties. *What virtue do we need to avoid our predominant sin? THAT should be the most frequent intention of our Rosary.*

2) We must know THE MYSTERIES not just as titles but in the fullness of their circumstances and meanings. Our Lady has asked us to work on this for at least fifteen minutes on five consecutive First Saturdays. She thus entices us into the joy of discovering the mysteries and how meaningful they can be to us. *The virtues we need are in the mysteries.*

It is only because they offer an easy way to seek the virtues we need that we suggested thinking of the seven gifts of the Holy Spirit, the seven capital sins, and the beatitudes.

As we progress in our use of the Rosary, in which Our Lady makes Her presence felt, helping us with the light from Her Immaculate Heart, we will find that the entire Rosary can serve in overcoming any specific fault or sin.

Once again, we recommend the book *Sex And The Mysteries,* not only for its own sake, but as an example of how the Rosary can become a most powerful instrument of holiness in our lives. Indeed, in that book, the author has dared to say: "I believe that no one could say the fifteen decades of the Rosary properly each day, and commit a mortal sin."

Experience has shown that to be true.

Most Powerful Help

After reading all the above, it must become evident that a special grace is needed to pray the Rosary well.

The children of Fatima received this in the light from our Lady's Immaculate Heart. We can receive it through wearing the Scapular and realizing that it is a sign of UNION with the Immaculate Heart of Mary. In giving us the Scapular, Our Lady promised us Heaven. And for purity of life while wearing the Scapular and saying the daily Rosary, WE MAY BE FREED FROM PURGATORY BY THE FIRST SATURDAY AFTER DEATH. Indeed, St. Alphonsus says: "If we do a little more, we may not go to Purgatory at all!" (See *Sign Of Her Heart*, chapter on Sabbatine Privilege.)

St. Claude de la Colombiere said that saints have told him that if he is devoted to Our Lady, he is sure of Heaven and knows that She is with him. But he says: to KNOW this, "I have only to reach out and TOUCH my Scapular."

Our Lady appeared for a final time in the skies of Fatima as Our Lady of Mount Carmel, holding the Scapular down to the world. Lucia said that this is because the Scapular is "our sign of consecration to Her Immaculate Heart," and she added these meaningful words:

"The Rosary and the Scapular are inseparable."

How can we pray to Our Lady effectively, unless we are aware that She is listening to every word?

The strings of the Scapular around our necks are like the arms of Our Mother embracing us, waiting for every word from our hearts and lips.

So, if we have an intention for every prayer, and if we know that Our Lady is listening, how can we wait until we have the occasion to say the Rosary again?

Only one thing would prevent us. It is sin. It is the lack of a sincere desire to have the virtues contained in this wonderful gift from Our Mother, such as purity.

Then the Rosary becomes more important than ever! And as we begin to say it, the virtues will come. With each bead, the Rosary will come more and more alive, more and more meaningful and powerful, lifting us through the Immaculate Heart of Mary to the heights of Divine Love, into the very Heart of Jesus.

"My Immaculate Heart will triumph," She said. And that is what Her triumph will be: Oneness in Their Hearts.

David Blum, an outstanding member of the World Apostolate of Fatima, had often asked our permission to tape a Rosary said with "spontaneous" meditations. When he came to the Blue Army Shrine in Washington, NJ, in 1990, with a large delegation from Erie, PA., he brought along a cameraman and equipment. With the aid of his close associate, Stan Kowalski, he taped the Rosary, which was said as a night prayer at the end of a very long and tiring day. The meditations included references to the events of the day, the gospel, and events planned for the next day.

Value of The Example

As was said in the previous pages, at first it may not be easy to say the Rosary this way. That is why we suggest the gifts of the Holy Spirit, the Seven Capital Sins, and the Beatitudes. All three make it possible to have a different intention for each and every Hail Mary.

Also, it is easier to pray this way in a group, even of two or three, with each person taking the intention for each of the prayers, or a person with special charism leading.

This adds ONLY ABOUT FIVE MINUTES to the time it takes to say the Rosary WITHOUT the intentions! Yet it makes all the difference in the world—the difference between "saying" the Rosary and "praying" it.

Importance of First Saturdays

Why did Our Lady ask: "Keep me company on the first Saturday of the month, meditating on one or more mysteries of the Rosary?" Is that not because She wants us, once a month, to take time out (only 15 minutes!) to practice?

"KEEP ME COMPANY," She said. She is present to us in a special way as we TRY once a month to LEARN about meditating on the mysteries. And the principles are "accidentally" exemplified in this tape.

AS WE THINK OF THE MYSTERIES, we may tie them to what Jesus said to us in the liturgy TODAY. He is the WORD of God, Incarnate. And the Word speaks to us EACH day in the liturgy. If you did not go to Mass today, do you remember the last sermon you heard, the last Gospel, the last Epistle? Is today a special feast, a day of special meaning or of special grace?

What are the conditions of the moment? What is happening to me TODAY? What graces do I need for what I shall do TOMORROW? Is there some special cross (even only being very tired and not FEELING like saying the Rosary)? Are there some wonderful gifts of God or of Our Lady for which I am grateful (like the Scapular and the Rosary, my health, my family)? Do I have some special NEED at the moment?

Really ALIVE

Even just using the gifts of the Holy Spirit, the Capital Sins, and the Beatitudes, we can make the Rosary extremely meaningful in our lives. But to make it REALLY alive to us, at this moment, we can have spontaneous intentions.

In the beginning, it is enough perhaps just to have the SAME intention for SEVERAL of the prayers. Intentions Our Lady especially loves to hear (as She told us at Akita) are for the Holy Father, Cardinals, Bishops, and priests. Another is: "Send forth the graces of your flame of love to all mankind." Or: "You have promised the triumph of Your Heart, let it begin with me!"

The Rosary comes alive and takes on its full dimension WHEN THE INTENTION for each prayer IS INSPIRED BY THE ACTUAL MYSTERY.

We cannot help mentioning again that there is an entire book (over 300 pages) just on praying the Rosary for PURITY. A whole new world of the Spirit is waiting to be explored when we "keep Our Lady company" in this marvelous devotion.

*Note: The Videotape referred to in this chapter may be obtained by writing to **Apostolate Divine Mercy, PO Box 630, Erie, PA 16512.***

CHAPTER FIFTEEN

CONCLUSION

In the first telecast after her miraculous cure (which took place during the recitation of the fourth mystery of the Rosary), Mother Angelica of EWTN was asked what she thought was going to happen as we entered the new millennium. To the surprise of many, she made two prophecies.

First, she expressed the belief that in the near future, God will grant to every living person an illumination of conscience—a moment in which everyone in the world would see themselves as God sees them.

Many expect this because it was prophesied by Blessed Anne Marie Taigi and others. It is expected to be a global moment of truth. And if there is enough grace in the world at that moment, the world could be saved by grace rather than by fire.

Next, she foresaw the coming triumph of the Sacred Hearts as a time when millions will be aware of the true presence of Our Lord in the Blessed Sacrament.

"The Time Has Come"

This hope I share with the reader, at the end of this little book, which that great apostle, Howard Dee, described as the most urgent message of our time.

During fifty years, I promoted the same message through the Blue Army. Although 25 million responded, today no single movement is enough. Everyone who believes must act.

"The time has come when words are not enough anymore," is the message issued by Vatican Radio in May, 1991, which so moved Ambassador Dee. And obviously, even more urgent are the succeeding words: "It is now necessary to act immediately if we wish that humanity may be able to see, besides the fire, light."

Is It Too Late for a Worldwide Response?

Naturally we want all humanity to respond, and immediately, to ALL that Our Lady asks of us. But experience shows that people are reluctant to sign a pledge even to wear the Scapular and to say a daily Rosary.

Based solely on what we can get across to them "immediately" even with the internet, pamphlets, TV bites, etc., how could we expect "immediately" to persuade millions to promise to say the Rosary and, even more, to make the First Saturdays?

In a moment, we will propose a simple, basic request. But first let us remember that we are not "starting from scratch." Millions know, through being told or through religious instinct, that our world is in need of correction. We can expect that our loving and merciful and just God would not permit the next generations to be swallowed up in the tidal wave of evil now engulfing much of the world.

Out of those millions aware that a Divine correction is likely, there are many millions who already *know* of the Divine interventions and warnings, some of which we have touched upon in these pages.

Finally, let us not forget that "elite corps"—those special few (and their number is increasing all over the world) who respond generously. Because of that small group, Our Lady said at Akita, She has already been able to hold back the chastisement.

There is a proliferation of articles, books, and tapes (audio and video) on this subject, including my own last three books previous to this one. And, God has given us a great Pope to lead us in this hour. Pope John Paul II wrote a unique book titled *Crossing the Threshold of Hope*, but he is in himself one of the greatest signs of hope.

In May of 1994, when he emerged from the hospital after four weeks of suffering, he said:

"I understood that I had to lead Christ's Church into the third millennium by prayer, by various programs, but I say that this is not enough. She must be led by suffering... The Pope has to be attacked, the Pope has to suffer, so that every family and the world may see that there is, I would say, a higher Gospel: the Gospel of suffering by which the future is prepared, the third millennium of families, of every family and of all families."

First Saturdays

As I was writing this, I received news that on the last First Saturday, due to extreme fatigue and another virus, he was unable to lead the First Saturday Rosary, as he did every month in the presence of thousands, and broadcast on Vatican Radio.

He had been leading the First Saturday devotions for so many years, month after month, that now his incapacity to do so, on this one occasion, was a reminder to the world of the example he set in leading us forward in the path mapped out for us by the victorious Queen of the World.

How many are following him?

We may sometimes feel hopeless because, as we look around us, there seem to be so few. And we keep hearing of so many scandals in the Church, and of an almost over-whelming loss of the sense of sin. In the United States, we were perhaps less shocked by the gross immorality and public lying of President Clinton than we were that three quarters of the population of the nation continued to support him.

So as we strive to be practical, we must ask what CAN we do, following the directions Our Lady has given us, to turn the tide? What was it the people of former Yugoslavia failed to do? What was it the people of Rwanda failed to do? Was there perhaps some ONE thing they might have done which would have made the difference?

One Simple, Basic Request

If we analyze all the messages Our Lady brings, we find one basic request to which we might expect millions to respond as they hear Her battle cry: "To save from destruction!" *It is Her request for consecration to Her Immaculate Heart.*

This is a decision to turn away from evil to good. It is a decision to choose God in a world denying Him. It is a tipping of the balance of those reaching out to God and those who reject Him.

Yes, but it is something even more.

The Mother of the Redeemer is on that balance to receive those who make this decision! She is there because that is God's merciful plan for us. As Blessed Jacinta said, "He has entrusted the peace of the world to Her."

Those names flying from all over the world to be placed in the maternal Immaculate Heart of the Queen of the World *empower Her.*

We are living the battle described in the Apocalypse between the Woman and the Dragon. We are living a crucial moment in the battle foretold in Genesis 3:15, which the angel showed at Akita to explain the 101 miracles of Our Lady's tears.

The decision of millions (yes, and even if there are less than many millions who will place their names in the heart of *the Woman*) adds weight in the scale of Divine Justice. In keeping with His Own plan for mercy to mankind, it empowers Our Lady and Queen to bring about the victory promised at Fatima: "Finally my Immaculate Heart will triumph. An era of peace will be granted to mankind."

A Last Hope

That is why the call to have millions send their names to be placed in the maternal Heart of Mary at the Queen of the World Center in the Fatima Castle may offer real hope.

As we mentioned previously, the sister of an outstanding American bishop received this inspiration while visiting the parish and tomb of St. John Vianney, in Ars, France. There she saw a statue of Our Lady in which the saint had placed the names of his parishioners in a parish which came alive and whose pastor became the official patron of all parish priests of the world.

So, she not only had a life sized statue of the maternal Immaculate Heart of Mary made for this purpose but she started a Queen of the World movement for signatures. Special Masses are to be said in major Marian shrines throughout the world for all who reply.

No money is asked. It is not even requested that those who offer to place their names in Our Lady's heart give an address unless they should want further communication. It is a purely voluntary and spiritual act.

Victorious Queen of the World

May every apostle of these latter times, as St. Grignion de Montfort describes them, be moved to participate! The saint said:

"It was through Mary that the salvation of the world was begun and it is through Mary that it must be consummated. Mary hardly appeared at all in the first coming of Jesus Christ. But in the second coming... Mary has to be made known and revealed by the Holy Ghost, in order that through her, Jesus Christ may be known, loved and served..."

This seems almost a specific prophecy of the devotion of Our Lady of All Nations, "who once was Mary."

Again, and this time definitely speaking as a prophet, the great Marian saint said further that in the latter times, "Mary must shine forth more than ever in mercy, in might, and in grace...terrible to the devil and his crew as an army ranged in battle, principally in the latter times when the devil, knowing he has but little time to destroy souls, will every day redouble his efforts and his combats. He will raise up cruel persecutions and will put terrible snares before the faithful servants and true children of Mary, whom it gives him more trouble to conquer than it does to conquer others."

He specifically foretold victory through the *totus tuus* apostles, including ultimate unity of Islam with Christianity.

As we pray that it is not too late, we pray that all Marian apostolates will vie with each other for the number of names to be placed in the maternal Immaculate Heart of the Lady of All Nations, the victorious Queen of the World, as we face the future looking not to possible destruction by fire, but to the light.

Note: To have your name placed in the maternal Immaculate Heart of Mary at the Fatima Castle, write to any of the QUEEN OF THE WORLD CENTER addresses listed on page ii.

APPENDIX I

EXCERPT FROM SEX AND THE MYSTERIES

Our Lady of Fatima said that MOST souls go to Hell because of sins of impurity. For that reason, the author has written a book of almost 300 pages applying the mysteries of the Rosary to chastity, according to one's state in life.

This book offers intentions for each prayer of all fifteen decades for persons who are single, for those who are married, and for children.

The following pages are an excerpt from **Sex And The Mysteries** *and contain the suggested intentions of the Joyful Mysteries, for those who are single.*

THE JOYFUL MYSTERIES

~The Annunciation~

And when the angel had come to her,
he said, "Hail, full of grace, the Lord is with
thee. Blessed art thou among women."
Luke 1, 28

Since God was going to become man, why did he not simply assume the body of a man, fully grown?

It was particularly difficult for the people of Israel in the year 30 to accept Christ because: "We know whence He comes!" They knew He was the son of a carpenter of Nazareth. They knew His relatives. Israel was a tiny nation, and the parents of Mary were well known. So how could He be the Messiah?

But since God chose to become man in the context of a family, why would he choose to be born helpless? And even before that, why should Divinity choose to unite itself to a tiny speck in a virgin's womb?

The world of now should stop and think of that for a moment. God, at the words of an angel spoken to a virgin, *united himself to an infinitesimal speck in the womb of a virgin and in this manner God became man.*

This was the greatest moment in history after creation. This was the moment of redemption. This was the moment of God's reunion with man. This was the moment of the re-establishment of the order of grace! This was the moment for which mankind had longed, crawling out of primeval darkness into which He had been plunged by original sin, crawling perhaps for thousands of years from an animal-like existence back towards this moment of light.

Let us fall on our knees before this mystery, *the dignity of parenthood!* Sex is wonderful and good because it places this miracle, this dignity of parenthood within the reach of most of us.

But let us tremble before the abuse of sex, which is a mortal sin because it is an abuse of this wonder of procreation, *by which the average man and woman touch upon the very mystery of God himself.*

(The following intentions to be inserted mentally in each Hail Mary after the words: "Pray for us sinners now...")

THOUGHTS after "Pray for us now..."

1. To respect the dignity of sex
2. To value virginity
3. To become pure like you and Joseph
4. To remain pure
5. To be overshadowed by the most High
6. To experience the reality of Christ in Communion as you did at the moment of the Annunciation
7. To perceive Jesus with a pure heart
8. For an increase of faith
9. To know that God's Graces is sufficient for me
10. Most Pure Heart of Mary, inflame with your love!

~The Visitation~

And Elizabeth was filled with the Holy Spirit,
and cried out with a loud voice, saying,
"Blessed art thou among women and
blessed is the fruit of thy womb!"
Luke 1, 41-42

We marvel at the very words of Our Lady to the angel, wondering how it was possible that God should become man through Her since She "knew not man." But Our Lady at once thought of Her promise to God of virginity.

There arose Our Lady's instinctive thought of her vow even at the moment that she was being told by an angelic vision that she was the one through whom the prayers and longings of mankind for so many centuries were to be fulfilled!

And then, the angel tells Mary that the sign of this great miracle, the sign of this great fulfillment for mankind, also concerns parenthood. Her cousin Elizabeth, well beyond the years of childbearing, was pregnant, and in her sixth month!

Scripture says that Our Lady "hastened" through the hill country to go to her cousin Elizabeth. This was certainly not because Our Lady doubted. She knew that God was within her, and that the words of the angel were true.

She knew too, that this "sign" was a mystery for people like you and me—people who do not adequately understand the dignity of sex, and the meaning of it—and who do not understand the dignity of the love of a husband for his wife and of a wife for her husband. And, *as she hastened through the hill country, it was already known to God that this would be the second mystery of the Rosary—which would carry its lesson down to this moment, to you and to me.*

When she came to the house of Elizabeth, the expectant mother of Saint John the Baptist cried out: "Whence is it that the mother of my Lord should come to me!"

It was revealed to Elizabeth instantly that Mary was the mother of the Messiah. And at that moment, she felt the six-month infant "leap in her womb." It was the moment of the sanctification of the yet unborn. How many thoughts flood to our minds before this great mystery!

We think of the murder of so many unborn infants today.

How much reparation is needed for sins against the dignity of parenthood!

And how did the privileged child of Elizabeth, the first in the world to "receive" Christ through Mary, come to his end? After having been the precursor of Christ, of whom Our Lord Himself said "no greater man was ever born..."

He died because of a promise made by a drunken king to an immodest dancer. He died because a woman committing public adultery was outraged that John the Baptist had appealed to the king to give her up! And after he was beheaded, the head of this "greatest man ever born of woman" was carried on a dish by the immodest dancer to her adulterous mother.

What a lesson in this day of mine!

Today, how many of us risk sullying our purity, our own respect for the divine dignity of parenthood, by attending sensual dances and spectacles! How often do we tolerate them on television, performances often almost identical to that which "pleased" the drunken king, and which—to teach us one of the most violent lessons of history—God permitted the beheading of the greatest man born to woman?

Saint John is in Heaven and is invoked every day in the opening of the Eucharistic Liturgy. The sun never sets on the invocation of his name in the confession of men's sins.

But the adulterous king died one of the most repulsive deaths in history: Stricken as he accepted to himself homage due only to God, his body consumed alive by worms. God, in becoming man to be our "Way, Truth, and Life," taught us many lessons. But, was any more drastic than this?

Greeting the mother of Saint John, we see the Immaculate Mother of the Incarnate God...we see the joy on their faces as the one bears beneath her Immaculate Heart the Savior of the world, and the other bears the child who will die in the defense of virtue. And Mary exclaims: "My heart rejoices in God my Savior!"

THOUGHTS after "Pray for us now..."

1. To avoid occasion of sin
2. To detest suggestive dances
3. Fearlessly to stand against public sin
4. To atone for sins of prevention of childbirth
5. To atone for sins of abortion
6. To control my eyes
7. To control my senses
8. To control my thoughts
9. To merit your Visitation in my own life
10. That my soul, too, may rejoice in God

~Birth of Jesus~

And she brought forth her firstborn son,
and wrapped him in swaddling clothes,
and laid him in a manger, because there
was no room for them in the inn
Luke 2, 7

Why did God call three kings for the long journey to Bethlehem? There may be many reasons, but one certainly is the value of holy companionship.

God said in the Garden of Eden, when He created both man and woman, that it was not good for man to be alone.

If we examine our consciences, is it not true that any sins we may have committed were either when we were alone, or when we were alone with one other person? Is it likely ever that we should commit a sin in the company of three well-disposed, sensible and honest people?

Holy companionship is a gift. How fortunate are those who, having the vocation to a special life of union to Christ for which they give up the privileges of parenthood and the intimacies of family life, have the fellowship of other holy persons who are traveling the same way, following the same star!

"And entering in, they found the child with Mary His mother." It is thus the Scripture describes the end of that blessed journey of the three holy companions.

Fortunate indeed the religious community that has sincere and good religious. Blessed indeed are those communities which have a superior who keeps the star shining brightly for all to see, for all to follow together, helping one another to their blessed goal: "the Child, with Mary His mother."

And those of us in the world, who do not have such chosen companions, may be blessed by God with beautiful friendships, if only we ask!

Nothing could be a greater, more practical aid to a pure life. It is possible to all of us is in the prayer groups which draw together souls following the same star, towards the same goal!

And what about all those crowds in Bethlehem that night of nights? Where were they? Why were only the poor shepherds called from the fields? Why only the three kings called from afar, from outside the nation?

Obviously because *only the clean of heart were called,* and persons who were not clean of heart are blind to stars lit by God, and deaf to voices of angels.

One of the tragedies of those who abuse sex is experienced in this life, immediately. The abuse of sex becomes absorbing. It blots out sensitivity to other beauty. It leaves us reveling in the noise of the city, while stars are shining and angels are singing and miracles are happening around us.

THOUGHTS after "Pray for us now..."

1. For the grace of good companions
2. For holiness in speech
3. To prefer and enjoy wholesome recreation
4. To follow you, Pure Star of the Sea!
5. To find you with Jesus today
6. To find Jesus with you today
7. To offer *purity of body as gold* to Jesus today
8. To offer *purity of thought as incense* to Jesus today
9. To offer *purity of words as myrrh* to Jesus today
10. In thanksgiving for purity

~The Presentation~

*And when the days of her purification
were fulfilled according to the Law of Moses,
they took him up to Jerusalem
to present him to the Lord.*
Luke 2, 22-23

Our Lady did not need purification. But this was one of the "sacraments" of the Old Testament, and Mary and Joseph set forth on the long journey to Jerusalem to be as close to the "holy of holies" as possible when they received the sacrament.

And we may not always need the purification of confession, but we must avail ourselves of the sacrament frequently especially that we may be guided.

This is one of the greatest gifts of Christ: His actual voice remaining with us through His priests. We are both purified and directed by the sacrament of confession. And at Fatima Our Lady required—if we wanted to obtain her great promise of having her come to us at the hour of death—that we go to confession at least once a month.

Then, Lucia explained that the purpose of this was: "to purify ourselves, and to renew our purpose." The purpose, of course, is that we remain chaste according to our state in life, aided by the devotions of the Rosary and the Scapular.

How can we remain pure when there are so many "grays," so many difficult decisions, without good confessions?

If Our Lady, who was all pure, bore the Infant Jesus up to the temple for purification, and there heard the priest foretell the greatest mystery of all Her coming life—that this Child will be set for the rise and fall of many and that Her own heart will be pierced by a sword—then can we not hope that when we go to confession, even if we do not feel the need, that with the proper faith and disposition we, too, may hear the directions for our life?

This is certainly a major benefit of the Sacrament and confession! It is the test of our sincerity and the fountain of our purification.

THOUGHTS after "Pray for us now..."

1. That I may have the grace of perfect contrition
2. To get to confession as soon as possible if I sin
3. For a good confession
4. To have the grace to make adequate reparation
5. To seek Jesus with a pure heart like you and Joseph
6. To find Jesus as my personal Savior
7. To be completely purified in my next confession
8. To accept difficult decisions of the confessor with joy
9. To esteem the sacrament of confession
10. To realize that in confession *it is Jesus Who forgives me*

~Finding Jesus in the Temple~
"Did you not know that I must be about my Father's business"
...and his mother kept all these things carefully in her heart.
Luke 2, 49-52

S ome may say that dancing is wrong, and others say it is good. Some may say one thing is permissible, while another will claim it to be sinful.

Individual doubts are resolved in the confessional. But to make a sensible and good confession, and to achieve a clean heart in our daily lives (particularly in the world at large), there must be some clear-cut principles to determine what is right and what is wrong.

This is the great lesson Our Lord taught to the world when He was only 12 years old. He separated Himself from His mother and father, and permitted them to seek Him in sorrow, while he "confounded" the doctors of the law by explaining the Scriptures to them.

He did this in a church, and when His parents found Him there He exclaimed—not for their benefit but for the millions who would discover these words again in the fifth mystery of the Rosary and in the readings of the Scripture: "Did you not know that I must be about My Father's business?"

Establishing His church twenty-one years later, He told the leaders of His church: "What you shall declare lawful on earth, shall be lawful in heaven; and what you shall declare unlawful on earth, shall be unlawful in heaven."

Thus, Christ Himself abides in His church, and is to be found there as always: "about My father's business" ...explaining the law, bringing us "up to date."

So when the successor of Peter issues an encyclical directing us in regard to this delicate matter of sex, about which all men today seem to disturbed, it is the voice of Christ.

We know this because of HIS own promise. "Behold I am with you all days..." (Matt. 28:20)

Our Lord Himself, who was God, set the example. Even though as a mere boy of 12, He was able to astound the most learned doctors of His time, but "He went down to Nazareth, and was subject to them."

Because one of the laws said that children should be obedient to their parents, and He—of His own choice—was a child! And so He was obedient.

Consider that again: He who made His parents, was obedient to them! He who was God became man, was obedient to men. He, whose parents would have obeyed Him had He asked, nevertheless did only what they asked.

This path of obedience is the one bright shining path which is joyfully followed by the clean of heart.

THOUGHTS after "Pray for us now..."

1. Always to seek Jesus
2. To listen to His voice in the church
3. To find Jesus with a pure heart
4. To be obedient to His voice
5. To uphold the law of God in the Sixth Commandment
6. To witness to that commandment before the world
7. To be subject to your requests at Fatima as Jesus was subject to you at Nazareth
8. For an increase in Faith
9. For confidence that God's Grace is sufficient for me
10. Most Pure Heart of Mary, inflame with your love!

Appendix II

PRAYERS TO THE FATHER TO INTRODUCE EACH MYSTERY

It is warmly recommended that brief prayers to the Father be said to introduce each mystery. At the beginning of the Rosary itself, immediately after the Creed (before the first *Our Father*), say:

O Eternal Father, we praise and thank You for sending Your Only Son into the world to redeem us, and for sending Him through Mary, that we might have both a Redeemer and a Mother.

Joyful Mysteries

1 - Dear Father, thank You for sending Your angel to ask Our Lady to become the Mother of Your Son and, at that same moment, our own Mother. Help us to understand this great mystery of Your Love!

2 - Dear Father, urged by the words of Your angel that *nothing is impossible to You*, Our Lady hastened to Her cousin Elizabeth. Grant, Father, that we too may live in the realization that to You nothing is impossible. Grant that we, like St. John the Baptist, may be sanctified at the sound of Our Lady's greeting.

3 - Dear Father, Your Provident Power moved the head of the great Roman Empire to issue an edict to fulfill Your Will that Jesus be born in Bethlehem, as foretold by Your prophet, and You sent a miraculous star to lead kings from afar. Lead us, O loving Father, and all the nations of the world, to Him Who came to us in a manger to reveal to us that You are Love.

4 - Dear Father, as Your daughter Mary and Her spouse St. Joseph presented Your Incarnate Word in the temple, You sent Your Holy Spirit upon Simeon and Anna to recognize Him, and to see into Mary's Immaculate Heart. Grant us the light of that same Holy Spirit.

5 - Dear Father, You willed that Your daughter Mary and Her spouse St. Joseph should endure the trial of separation from Jesus, and the joy of having Him return to Nazareth to abide with them. Grant that we may endure the trial and have Jesus abide with us.

Sorrowful Mysteries

1 - Dear Father, in His agony in the garden, Jesus cried out: "Not My Will but Thine be done!" O good Father, that I may ever accomplish Your Holy Will! Thy kingdom come! Thy Will be done!

2 - Father, we are appalled to see Your Divine Son bound and scourged, as He is "bound" in our tabernacles as a Prisoner of Love, scourged by our indifference and even by sacrilege. Grant, through the intercession of Our Lady, that we may console our Prisoner of Love!

3 - Father, they mocked the kingship of Your Divine Son with a crown of thorns. We affirm His kingship! May He reign in our lives! Thy Kingdom come!

4 - Father, we believe that Calvary is present at every Mass. To assist well at our next Mass, we wish to follow in the footsteps of the sorrowful and Immaculate Heart of Mary on the road to Calvary where, by His death, Jesus opened for us the gates to Your Kingdom.

5 - The night before He died, He said: "When you see Me, you see the Father." Dying, He said: "Into Your Hands I commit My Spirit." O good Father, in the passion of Jesus, may we recognize the greatness of Your love and Mercy. By the intercession of the sorrowful and Immaculate Heart of Mary at the foot of the cross, may many souls be saved. May You be honored and loved in all the world!

Glorious Mysteries

1 - Dear Father, the first recorded words of Your Divine Son, after His resurrection, were: "Do not touch Me, I have

not yet ascended to My Father!" He reminded us, as He had three days before at the Last Supper, that He came from You. Confirm us in the hope of our own resurrection, to be with You forever.

2 - Ascending to You, dear Father, He said that You would send the Holy Spirit to make all things known to us. He left His Mother behind to gather with the faithful in prayer, as we do now.

3 - Father, You kept the promise Jesus made as He ascended to You. You sent the Holy Spirit upon Our Lady and the apostles. Grant, beloved Father, through Her intercession, that we may receive the gifts of Your Spirit.

4 - With what joy, Father, You received Your daughter Mary assumed into Heaven! We are told that in this joy all Purgatory was emptied. By Her intercession, grant relief to the holy souls and final contrition to all the dying! And grant, by Her motherly intercession, that we shall one day be with You and the saints forever in Heaven.

5 - Eternal Father, we rejoice to live in this age of mercy when You have entrusted the peace of the world to Mary, our loving Mother! We hail Her as our Queen. May She use us for the triumph of Your Kingdom!

Beautiful Prayer To God the Father

In the last year of the twentieth century (1999), the year of special honor to God the Father, millions came to know of the beautiful revelations given by God the Father to Mother Elizabeth Eugenia Ravasio in the early part of the century, and approved in 1945. *Each invocation lends itself to use in the Rosary.*

At the heart of these revelations is a prayer, which begins by reminding our loving Father that, AT EVERY MOMENT, and WHEREVER WE ARE, He is *waiting and expecting* us to turn to Him.

So often we are aware that God is everywhere and that He knows our every thought. But how often do we realize that *no matter where we are, under whatever circumstances, and at whatever time,* He is loving us, caring for us, and waiting for us to turn to Him!

That is the first wonderful truth of which He reminds us as we begin this prayer. Then He tells us *how* to pray in a manner which almost *compels Him* to grant what we ask.

Following is the main part of this wonderful prayer, followed by a brief glance at its greatness.

The Prayer

My Father in Heaven, how sweet it is to know that You are my Father and that I am Your child! Teach me to surrender myself to You like a baby in its mother's arms.

Father, You know everything, You see everything, You know me better than I know myself. You can do everything, and You love me.

Since it is Your wish that I should always turn to you, I come with confidence to ask You, *together with Jesus and Mary...* (*request the favor you desire*).

For this intention, *uniting myself to Their Most Sacred Hearts,* I offer You all my prayers, my sacrifices and mortifications, all my actions, and a greater fidelity to my daily duties.*

Give me the light, the grace, and the power of the Holy Spirit!

Strengthen me in this Spirit that I may never lose Him, never sadden, never cause His gifts to lessen in me.

Father, I ask this in the name of Jesus, Your Son! And you, O my Jesus, open Your Heart and take into It my own and, together with Mary's, offer it to our Divine Father, obtaining for me the grace I need.

Divine Father, that you may be known, honored, and loved by all men! (3 times)

With Jesus and Mary

In this beautiful prayer, Our Father has us come to Him WITH JESUS AND MARY. We come to Him not as sinful, hesitant, unworthy children of Adam and Eve. We come to Him as the children of Mary, redeemed by Jesus.

Then we ask Him for what we desire.

Those three elements (He is waiting, we come with Jesus and Mary, and we ask) are the first parts of the prayer. Now comes the most beautiful part. The Father tells us to make an offering for the intention we have voiced, *in union with the Sacred Hearts:*

"For this intention, uniting myself to Their Hearts ..."

We have gone to the Father in the first place, "with Jesus and Mary." With THEM, in a oneness with Them as Mother and Redeemer, we have placed our petition before Him. Now *He teaches us to continue our prayer IN UNION WITH THEIR HEARTS.*

This is not just a prayer. *This is a way of vital spiritual living.*

In Union with Their Sacred Hearts

In union with Their Hearts, the Father invites us to offer *sacrifices, mortifications, prayers, actions, and greater fidelity to our daily duty,* mentioning if possible one aspect of our duty, which we promise at this moment to fulfill with greater fidelity.

The asterisk at this point in the prayer indicates that if we are saying this prayer as a novena, we should add; "I promise to be more generous, especially in these nine days, in a given circumstance, to such and such a person.."

This would indicate that the fidelity to duty which especially pleases our Father is the duty of love, particularly in the family.

The Holy Spirit

As we say this prayer, day after day, we may wonder *what sacrifices* today? We might think of the greatest of all, the Mass. *What mortifications?* We may think of at least some little thing of which we will deprive ourselves today. *What prayers?* The Rosary? *What actions?* All of them! And to what duties are we lacking in fidelity?

One would think that the greatness of this gift from our Father, this magnificent and powerful prayer, was by now exhausted. **But better is still to come.**

What sacrifices SHALL we make? What mortifications? What actions and which of our daily duties do we most neglect? The Father now tells us to ask Him:

"Give me the light, the grace, and the power of the Holy Spirit!" with the added prayer that we will never be parted from the Holy Spirit, that we will never sadden Him, that we will never cause the gifts He brings to diminish in us.

Oh, what a beautiful and powerful prayer! It is a prayer NEVER to commit serious sin. It is a prayer recognizing that we are temples of the Holy Spirit and asking that we never sadden Him by venial sin and never reject His great gifts of wisdom, knowledge, piety, understanding, perseverance, and fortitude, which He desires to bring to us and make effective in us at every moment.

So, is this the end of this wonderful prayer, this wondrous gift of our Heavenly Father to our age? No, STILL THE BEST IS TO COME!

Now, after asking for His Holy Spirit, He tells us to add:

My Heart offered together with Mary's!

"I ask this in the name of Jesus, Your Son!"

Then our loving Father instructs us to ask IN A WAY HE HIMSELF CANNOT REFUSE in what seems to many the most beautiful part of the entire prayer:

"And You, Jesus, open Your Heart and place in It my own and, together with Mary's, offer it to our Divine Father!"

One can almost see Our Dear Lord take that little black speck of my heart and place it into the furnace of His Heart which contains the flame of the love of *our* Mother. One can see the speck transformed in Her Heart as Jesus offers both, out of the flame of His Love, to His Father.

Asking again that our request be heard we add three times: *"That the Father may be known, honored, and loved by all mankind!"*

As we say his, perhaps we will think of those who do not know God at all, who are estranged and do not know He loves His prodigal children and awaits them, persons who deny Him, many of whom are only vaguely aware of Him, so very many whom He longs to be as close to as He is to us but, as Our Lady said at Fatima, are separated "because there is no one to make sacrifice and to pray for them."

Inexhaustible Beauty

Books have been written about the Lord's Prayer, the prayer to the Father taught to us by Jesus. Books could also be written about this prayer taught to us by the Father to come to Him in the Hearts of Jesus and Mary.

The more one prays in these beautiful words taught to us by our own loving, Heavenly Father, the more their richness seems inexhaustible. Just the words "in union with Their Sacred Hearts" expresses a whole lifetime of devotion of saints like St. John Eudes... a devotion now coming into full flower.

And what more could we ask of Jesus that he open His Heart and take into it our own to be offered, *together with Mary's*, to our Father?

And yet, like the Lord's Prayer, even said slowly and deliberately this prayer taught by Our Father takes less than one minute!

*Note: For further information see **God Our Father Edition**, Queen of Peace, 6111 Steubenville Pike, McKees Rock, PA, 15136.*

For further details, we urgently recommend the following books by John Haffert:

1) HER OWN WORDS TO THE NUCLEAR AGE includes the entire memoirs of the visionary of Fatima as well as quotes from her most important letters and interviews.

2) TO PREVENT THIS explains the response which can prevent the annihilation of entire nations.

3) SIGN OF HER HEART, on the Scapular.

4) MEET THE WITNESSES, on the Miracle of the Sun.

5) SEX AND THE MYSTERIES, on the Rosary.

6) HER GLORIOUS TITLE describes how the basic pledge of Fatima places us on the ascent of Carmel, the ascent to holiness.

7) YOU, TOO! GO INTO MY VINEYARD! for lay apostles and saints of today.

8) THE WORLD'S GREATEST SECRET on the Eucharist. Sold over 100,000 copies.

9) THE MEANING OF AKITA contains all the actual words spoken by Our Lady at Akita, including the third secret of Fatima *with the renewed prophecy of annihilation of nations if the response to the message of Fatima is ignored now in this post-consecration period.* (Note: The pastoral letter approving the apparitions of Akita was released at the time of the third sign: the collegial consecration of March, 1984.)

10) NOW THE WOMAN SHALL CONQUER, based on the signs and means of Our Lady's final triumph.

11) NIGHT OF LOVE, on the first Friday/Saturday vigils. New edition.

Other books by the same author include:

DEAR BISHOP! memoirs written at the insistence of the author's bishop.

THE DAY I DIDN'T DIE, extended memoirs written in 1998.

EXPLOSION OF THE SUPERNATURAL, "Send NOW Your Holy Spirit over the earth!"

THE BROTHER AND I, story of the vision which led to a worldwide Fatima apostolate.

FINALLY RUSSIA, when Our Lady appeared over Red Square.

THE HAND OF FATIMA, Christian-Muslim division and Mary in the Koran.